Robert Griffiths

# COCKNEY IN CORBIERE

Bloomington, IN  Milton Keynes, UK

*AuthorHouse™*
*1663 Liberty Drive, Suite 200*
*Bloomington, IN 47403*
*www.authorhouse.com*
*Phone: 1-800-839-8640*

*AuthorHouse™ UK Ltd.*
*500 Avebury Boulevard*
*Central Milton Keynes, MK9 2BE*
*www.authorhouse.co.uk*
*Phone: 08001974150*

*© 2006 Robert Griffiths. All rights reserved.*

*No part of this book may be reproduced, stored in a retrieval system, or transmitted by any means without the written permission of the author.*

*First published by AuthorHouse 8/8/2006*

*ISBN: 1-4259-2709-2 (sc)*

*Printed in the United States of America*
*Bloomington, Indiana*

*This book is printed on acid-free paper.*

# CHAPTER ONE

If inspiration can come from strange places, this was one of the strangest: Sharon's mouth. I had walked into work, a jeweller's shop in the roughest part of London, where she pretended she was a shop assistant.

Everyday I had to get past her short body wedged between the wall and the counter; she determined to "ave a word', hoping to impress me with some idea or deed.

This Saturday she changed my life:

"Me and 'Arry are gonna immigrate to Spain," her squeaky, cockney voice screeched, hurting my ears.

The word 'Spain' flashed a series of hot, happy, careless, blue-skied memories through my head.

She stood frozen against the counter, smiling up at me.

"What are *you* going to do down *there*?" I said through a stinging hangover.

"My 'Arry's a qualified football coach!"

'Just what the Spanish *don't* need,' I thought, 'your 'Arry screaming at them in a cockney accent even a Londoner, born *sitting* on the Bow Bells, wouldn't understand a word the stupid git was saying!'

"What about learning Spanish?" I said
"We're gonna learn that goin' daan in the mota," she said with a shrug.

I looked into those glassy eyes; was she serious? I realised she was. She looked at me for approval. I dropped my shoulders and scowled at her, turned round, walked through the stinking curtain that separated the shop from the kitchen, went over to the gas stove, picked up the kettle that was on it and told it what a fucking idiot she was.

Sharon was small and dark; the bone structure of her head had once held a pretty face. Still not old, she looked gaunt. Her dress sense she invented, nobody would want to admit they designed what she wore. Everyday she looked completely different, there was no theme to what she put on. Her favourite colours were purple, brown and pink. Sometimes she put all the different colours together and looked like a crazed patchwork quilt; other times, she looked like a flattened ball of candy floss; on her darker mornings, a muddy pond stomped around the jewellery shop, frightening the customers. She was cockney and not proud of it. She had completed courses on psychology and not understood a word, been away on 'How-to-paint-like-Monet' holidays and attended pointless night classes. She tried to learn sign language; she practised until her bony hands throbbed, then gave that up to study the classic Greek authors during her tea break. At lunch time she sat in a corner of the shop's kitchen with ear phones on, listening to Linguaphone.

One morning, tightly wedged against the wall, her over painted face was trying to look blasé. She informed me she had become a Samaritan:

"'Dem physiology lessons 'ad been very 'andy!"

I felt even sorrier for those poor souls pouring their lives down the telephone line. A little bit of knowledge wasn't a dangerous thing, it was deadly.

Except for her dress sense, she was a poor mirror image of myself.

I think I hated her.

She regarded me as educated and cultured because I read books and big newspapers, but I was as cockney as she, and less educated than most.

Jewellery shop? If you could call it that! Looked like the inside of a shabby, daytime drinking club, the ones that opened when pubs closed: old ruby-red flock wallpaper, tatty hand-made counters, sticky brown carpet, the air full of cigarette smoke and yesterday's BO.

A full-length photograph of Cliff Richards overlooked the shop. What Cliff had to do with a jeweller's shop only the bi-sexual manager understood.

There was nothing else inside, only the staff perched around the never-ending counter like bored ravens. All the shop's jewellery was hung on hundreds of numbered trays displayed in the window. Each tray was covered with a claret coloured mock-velvet cloth. They were all hooked to a powerfully illuminated display rack that completely filled up the extensive window. The reflected, golden light brightened the dilapidated street and glowed on the faces of the craving shoppers. Unknowing customers eventually gained access to the shop, expecting to see ticking clocks and watches, silver pots and cruet sets. Instead, they stood on tacky carpet, staring at the twilight zone.

The main source of the shop's decaying BO stench was the oily, fat, gross doorman. He sat behind the elongated counter facing a glass box that the customers had to navigate themselves through to get into the shop. The tools of his trade were two buttons that operated buzzers which then opened the locks on the doors; they allowed the customer entry into the shop. The first buzzer opened the door that let the customer into the glass box. Once the door was closed behind them, the doorman pressed the second button which opened the next door, letting the customer into the shop. Once inside, the customers had to manoeuvre themselves across the sea of gooey carpet. The confusion of finding themselves in the house of horrors wasn't helped by the staff who completely ignored anything that looked like a shopper:

"Serve? And miss a bit of gossip?!"

When the customer looked inquisitively at the only person facing him, the doorman, everybody got the same instructions from him. He would jab his stubby, sticky finger at the flock of ravens and say:

"I know nuffink. I let 'em in, I let em owt. Ask one of that lot."

That's all he did, from eight until six, six days a week, no lunch break, no holidays. When you walked passed him, he stunk of shit.

The few customers that survived this ordeal had to wait until one of the jabbering, cross-armed ravens looked over her shoulder and croaked:

"There's naffink inside the shop; all the gold's inna windas luv. Go back awtside, look inna winda, when you see wot you wont, remember the tray numba it's on, come back in 'ere and I'll get that tray awt for ya."

On their return into the shop the dazed shopper inevitably forgot their tray number. They were told by an exasperated crow:

"Gaa back awtside an' 'av annaver look, an' nis time daan't forget ya numba!"

On their third journey, stood in the glass tardis and waiting for that second buzzer, you could see the frightened buyer mouthing the tray number to himself. The doorman would keep his tacky finger off the second buzzer until the poor shopper's face started to turn to panic as his twenty second recall ran out and his lips stopped moving. The doorman's fat, greasy body would wobble in a sadistic chuckle;

"I'will let 'im in now 'e's forgot it again."

By the time they reached the counter, their whimpering, forgetful apology said it all.

The experienced raven was usually sympathetic.

"You've forgot it again luv, ain't ya? You go awtside, I'wll walk round to the winda, and when you see me frew it, point at the tray ya wont an' I'wll get it awt for ya."

On her way to the display window, the raven would shake her disapproving head at the doorman. His response would be to turn his chunky palms to the ceiling and, with a look of angelic innocence, say through his plump, grinning lips:

"What?"

On busy days this pantomime could be acted out ten times simultaneously.

The colony of ravens usually numbered around ten. They ranged from illiterate teenagers, who were usually planning for early pregnancy so they could retire and be given a nice council flat with fitted half-caste baby, to old crones who couldn't afford to retire. Some were housewives who had been released from their domestic duties, their children were grown up enough to push their own half-caste baby up and down the high street. Then there were the ones who, for years, kept up the pretence:

"I'm only workin' 'ere until I get a proper job."

They never did.

Some of them packed their knickers with golden trinkets which they exchanged for a weekend of Ecstasy.

Some were out of work teachers who said they only took the job:

"..to see what the real world was like."

There was always one young boy. He was the manager's. He usually lasted a few months, by which time the predatory, bi-sexual alcoholic who was supposed to run the shop had his way with him. Or not. The young buck was always regretfully sacked, and there was always another one, from the long line queuing outside the local youth hostel, to take his place. And then there was Sharon.

The girls who worked here were immune to violence.

At the weekend there was the usual pub punch-up; they spent most of Monday morning delightfully reliving the gory details over 'a nice cup of tea.'

Domestic bloodshed, however, was more serious; the women workers whispered and displayed their cuts and bruises in select groups behind the loo door.

Three times in the last two years the shop had been held-up; drugged-up loonies pointing shotguns into the girls' faces, screaming at them to load the jewellery from the windows into bags being pushed at them. The girls filled the obligatory black bin liners with gold, *slowly*, doing their best to look as surly as possible.

During the last hold-up, a huge dread-locked berserker brandishing a rusty, old, useless shotgun was screaming instructions at the cowering Doorman. From behind the counter, a bored, young, lazy, female voice said:

"Take it easy luv! No need to shout, is dere?"

I stepped through another mouldy curtain, this one separated the shop from my workshop.

'She's going to learn to speak Spanish driving down in the mota; she can't make herself understood in English!'

Up in the shop it was morning tea. The staff were sitting around the counter, reading the tabloids. I could hear their grating voices; they were discussing an article in one of the daily papers. From the story, they came to the conclusion that Elvis was alive.

"Yeah for sure."

"Cawse he is."

"Maast be."

"Beyond a shadow of a dawt."
"Definitely."
" Never dawted it."

I could imagine the doorman's suety head nodding like the toy dog in the back of his car.

I had a workshop in the cellar of this place, repairing jewellery most people would have thrown away. There were no windows, no ventilation, just my work bench and assorted bits of machinery needed to repair and make jewellery. I never cleaned it, the place was stacked with dust gathering materials I had no use for and no intention of throwing away. The floor was grim encrusted concrete, the walls covered in wallpaper an ambitious shop keeper put up during the war. The deal I made with the man who used to own the shop suited us both at the time. If the shop looked like losing a sale because a piece of jewellery didn't fit, one of the staff brought it down to me, I altered it, the girl took it back up to the shop, gave it to the buyer, shoved the money in the till and everybody was happy. For supplying this unique service, I had the workshop free of rent. All the jewellery repairs that came through the glass door were mine. I worked from eight thirty in the morning 'til eight o'clock at night, six days a week and made a fortune.

One Monday morning, as I was creeping from the kitchen to the workshop with a mug of tea during this ritual paper-reading/ tea-drinking session, I watched them as they discussed an article in the Sunday Sport.

One of the girls thought the article so important she'd even brought it in to show to the other ravens.

"'Ere, look, I towld ya! It *is* true! Look at this!"

She slid the paper round the counter for everyone to look at, so, of course, they completely ignored it.

She scooped the tabloid up, stood up and started to read out loud from the front page:

"Nahbody believed me! But I know wot I saw! It says it 'ere in black and white: 'LORD LUCAN SPOTTED IN SPANISH BAR DRESSED AS A FLAMENCO DANCER!' I told ya! Me an' Fred saw him last year when we was on 'oliday! Only that time he was dressed different; he looked like a bull fighter."

The flatulent Doorman burped and said:

"Well, if it says it in da paper, it's gotta be da trufh! She was rite all along! Lord Lucan's still alive! Who'd believe it?"

Now, through the curtain, I could still hear their voices; they were deliberating the reappearance of Elvis.

Apparently he had a job as a petrol station assistant in Peckham.

I fell down onto my stool, their words exhausting me.

My head dropped into my hands.

"He can't ave! My uncle, he works in nat garege, and he's never seen 'im!" one of them squawked.

My head dropped between my knees.

The Monday after that inspirational word, emigrate, was spat out of Sharon's mouth, I was soaking in my new bath with my new baby daughter, the tub big enough for me, both my daughters and the wife. This was the only time of the day I had them altogether. The bath was Swedish, expensive like everything in this house.

Money well spent.

"Don't forget the doctor's appointment this morning," said the wife entering the bathroom with a tray of breakfast goodies.

I had been to see the doctor two weeks before as I was concerned about two lumps that had appeared on my hip. I was very surprised when he took my temperature and some blood, then asked me to undress. He listened to my chest and heart, tested my reflexes, then told me to put my clothes back on again. As he was a poof, just thought he fancied me.

"Come back in two weeks time," he said.

Good job the wife remembered the appointment.

Back in his surgery a few hours later, with the test results on his desk, he didn't look happy.

"Cheer up, doc! Can't be *that* bad!"

He ignored me, stood up and started to talk down to me:

"The reason I gave you a complete examination two weeks ago was because you said you'd lost weight recently."

I had said something like 'the bathroom scales always showed a different figure'.

He continued:

"After which I asked you to describe your daily routine to me."

Well, I had described it to him, then told him about the lunatic Christmases, watched his face become very grave, so watered the story down a bit.

"Robert he said with genuine concern, "if you continue working the hours you do, with the stress you're under, for *another* year, it will be very difficult for me. There's a *serious* chance you could become *very* ill."

Afterwards, driving to work, thinking about how concerned he sounded, I felt bad about the poof bit.

As well as repairing the jewellery for the shop, part of my daily routine consisted of driving around the busy parts of south London, collecting work from other jewellers. I had to stop the car as near to the shops as the parking wardens would allow, rush in, collect the work, then race back out again, all the time hoping the muggers wouldn't get me. I managed to get this extra work by telling the shop owners I'd return the repaired jewellery in 24 hours.

I had to get around the shops as quickly as possible. There was always so much to do; I had no partner to help me with the work and never had a day off sick.

Ever.

That wouldn't have been so difficult, but unfortunately the repairs that came into our shop had to be done whilst the customers waited. This really stressed me out, especially as the assistants usually got the instructions wrong. This left the client doing his nut in the middle of the shop and I would then be asked to come up to the shop to 'sort it out.'

Sorting out a variety of black or white goggled-eyed smack-heads who threatened you with death or maiming had been a daily routine for years.

Then, Christmas arrives. Last year was so busy I got on all fours and howled like a dog.

There was the night job as well, but I won't go into that.

A new baby, cricket or football on Sundays, pubs, restaurants and smoke-filled jazz clubs, snooker once a week, football training twice a week, work six days a week; all this accompanied by gallons of beer, wine, and scotch'n'coke. The tax man hadn't sent me a bill for years so I never paid any. I had no social security number and didn't want one. I drifted unconsciously out of the state system as a boy and had no idea how to get back in. I worked hard and paid my bills. My mortgage was bent; that, and the fear of big brother brushing aside the workshop curtain to cart me off, helped the pints fly down. I dreaded sleep; the nightmares were real. The hangover always woke me before the alarm clock.

To disguise my alienation I dressed and acted as if I went hunting at weekends. I had the perfect wife and children, new car and posh house, but I felt like a gypsy camped next to the M 4. The only way seasons affected me were to force the doors of the hot wine-bar ajar.

I loved London; it was loving me to death.

Turning this lot over, I reckoned the doc had a point, but I wasn't going to jump in front of this rolling ball.

Ownership of the shop had changed recently, which didn't help. The old owner had been a friend. He'd sold out to city wiz-kids who were seduced by the promise of tax-free cash from disposable wage earners. My mate lied to them, but as they had only paid him in over-valued shares, then made him the company director of a firm that didn't really exist, they didn't really care.

Not long before this awesome partnership, he was the most wanted criminal in Britain.

I thought they deserved each other.

The wiz-kids were sweeping through the shop making new rules and regulations. There was a new one for me everyday. All the plans for me were just different ways for them to get their hands on my takings. I knew they were doing it because the promised cash hadn't appear, so now they wanted mine.

I reckoned, as my mate was still involved as a company director with these idiots, I was safe.

To make sure, I gave him a buzz

"I won't let them touch ya, nor the workshop, mate. Always look after me own, not to worry! Everything's all right. I'll have *a word*, make sure those dickheads keep off your back!"

He said all this too quickly, then the line went dead.

There was none of his usual banter or jokes. He didn't ask after the family, he couldn't get off the phone quick enough.

'He's a lying bastard,' I thought, 'they've found out about his crooked past, he's only keeping me sweet until he robs them blind then fucks off. There's nothing he's going to do to help.'

After careful consideration that took about ten seconds, I decided to try and set up a new workshop elsewhere, screw every penny I could out of this place, then piss off, hoping to keep the delivery business going at the same time.

Phoned my first boss for some advice. He had recently told me he'd had to slow down as he was now eighty, so reduced his working week to four days. I didn't ask how many hours a day.

I had completed a five-year apprenticeship under him. Five years of slavery, so I reckoned he could spare me five minutes on the phone. Asked him the best place to build another workshop.

He answered, in his strong, Jewish, London accent:

"The Thatcher years are over, my son, business has collapsed. Our trade always suffers first. People have stopped buying luxury goods; they put their broken jewellery in a box, and then wait for things to pick up before getting it repaired. So if you have no money to see you through the next few years, *and you don't*, get out and do something else!"

He was right, the old goat was always right. There was going to be a lot more trouble, but what I wanted to know was how much? And how long would it last?

"A recession?" I whimpered

"Worse. I just told *you*; business has collapsed! A Recession? This is not recession! I've been through three of them! This is depression! I've got loads of money and *I* will have trouble getting through this one. *You've* got no chance."

He was getting angrier and more flustered; I was getting fed up with him.

"Yeah, yeah, alright! So how long will it last?"

"How long is a bit of string?" I could see him shrugging

"Got any ideas then?"

"None."

Mumbled something like 'thanks for those kind words' and put the phone down.

A few days after that informative telephone call, one of the slime-ball wiz-kids came into my workshop. He stood beside me with his arms crossed defiantly, legs apart, smelling of Paco Rabanne. He tried to look serious and adamant. I kept working.

He lowered his voice and started to inform me that the new company had decided to take over my business and put me on a wage.

"How much?" I grunted.

He choked out a figure less than a third of what I took in a day. I stood up, walked towards him, leant down, then pushed my face into his.

"You know that's not enough to feed my fucking budgerigar! Do you think I've worked my bollocks off all these years for you to come in here and take the business off me?" my face was pushing him back against the wall, "you think you can fuck my life up as easily as that, then just walk out of here, go home to your poxy little house, cuddle your ugly misses, then go to bed and fall peacefully asleep? If you even try this shit, one night, you'll open your front door, and *I* will be waiting for you, sat in *your* living room. Then, I'll fuck *your* life up forever. Now piss off, you soppy cunt!"

I knew the staff would have their ears pressed against that curtain, so I said all this in a bloodthirsty whisper.

He scurried through the curtain.

They dropped the idea of putting me on a wage.

I was finding it hard to concentrate on my work. I spent hours in the workshop, daydreaming about Sharon's word.

Emigrate.

The thought of leaving all this lunacy felt good, felt warm, if only I could manage it! Bunk off, leave all this shit, change everything, get away, before it destroys me.

Sunshine, blue skies, no stress!

Just the wife, the kids and me!

It made no difference those suited cunts up there were leaving me alone. I knew it was time to move on.

Putting everything together (the doctor's advice, my business and what my first boss told me), I reckoned I had to earn a living somewhere else if I was going to pay the mortgage.

Now, that inspirational word from Sharon was haunting me:

Emigrate.

But how?

In my youth, I bummed around Europe, lived in a couple of Scandinavian countries for a few years, but with a family, it would be harder.

Go somewhere where the living's cheap and I can be alone with my family.

Rent the house out to pay the mortgage and sail away!

That's the thing to do!

Get away from this existence entirely, no worrying, a new, *clean* adventure.

A year away.

Then come back, refreshed, bronzed and happy, ready to try again.

Paperback [] amzuk_chl 3.19+0.00 UL
COCKNEY IN CORBIERE - griffiths, Robert

I lived on the opposite side of London from where I worked. There was a big cultural difference between work life and home life. At work they thought me a snob because of where I lived. The area where I was born, and still lived, was being bought up by people who wouldn't open the door of our local pub. The houses had become expensive, so had our neighbours. Candle-lit dinner parties replaced 'Knees up Mother Brown'. Most of the newcomers were friendly, unsure of their new environment; cosmopolitan Londoners a substitution for their shire-county up bringing. To them, the Capital was only a means to an end, they had their family and friends elsewhere, the cockney accent suspicious to these swede-bashers raised on Radio Four and 'Only Fools and Horses'. Neighbourhood watch was the new game; I played the old game with a cleaver in the cupboard. I tried to help them settle; they thought I was planning to nick their silver.

After the first rush of amiability, the cross-pavement waving stopped. Then they bolted their doors and barred their windows. Shortly after, men in white overalls appeared to attach burglar alarms like single measles's spots on the façades of their houses. For most of my life, I had only seen the posh parts of Chelsea through sparkling clean glass; still no invitation came to sit on the other side of the window with no net curtains. From my sofa, I watched our neighbours' faces reflecting the flickering light from their candles whilst laughing at a clever remark. We were never asked to reflect the light or hear the joke. Our invitations to dine were met with an amused refusal, neighbourly recognition ultimately reduced to a nod.

Most of my friends and family were to move away, unable to resist the high prices houses would command. They became the new swede-bashers, yearning for a lifestyle that no longer existed.

Impossible to go back.

It was Saturday morning. I didn't want to go to work. I had to drag myself to the car. Started the engine and limped off, feeling miserable, bored and hung-over. I drove through Chelsea, arrived at Wandsworth bridge and wanted to turn back. I wanted to walk through Richmond park today, not shit myself driving through the Peckham estate.

I followed my usual shortcut; the houses and tower blocks became more and more grey and seedy, the buildings darker and scarier, the smells more acrid. Here, all the shops I had to pass sold things I'd never want to buy. The thread of desperation grew longer as I drove further from home. I wound my window up, tuned the radio to 'Sounds of the Sixties,' and day dreamed about escape.

Arrived at the shop, parked the car and went in.

Sharon was waiting; she asked me where I was going on holiday this year. I knew this question would lead me down a cul-de-sac, so tried to shut her up.

"Taramasalata." I said.

Nothing shuts Sharon up:

"Oh, luvely! Me and 'Arry went daan there last yer! D'ya go in nat'bar run by the lesbians? Luvely couple! Day've *never* 'eard of closing time out there! Me and 'Arry used to sit and drink 'til we fell off our f-in' bar stools! Burnt to a crisp we were."

She looked thoughtful, then her mouth started again:

"Could we pass frew it on our way daan to Barcelona?"

"You'll get a bit sticky if you do!" I answered.

She folded her arms defensively, leant back slightly, looked me in the eyes and said:

"Why?"

"Where is Taramasalata?" I glared at her

"You get on a plane, when you get off, you're dere, ain't ya?"

"Where are *you* now?" I said, learning on the counter

"Peckham!" she said and glared back

"Why don't you put a bit of Peckham on your Taramasalata add a touch of Lewisham, then eat it for diner tonight," I said, pushing the curtain open.

"Touchy ain't he today?" I heard her say to no-one.

Work was difficult. I had made my mind up to get out of this place. I spent weeks racking my brains, desperately trying to think of somewhere to go.

'No-one emigrates to *Spain* anymore,' I kept telling myself, 'no need for that; just get away for a bit.'

Couldn't go too far in case anything went wrong with the tenants renting the house. But not Spain; that would be too hot for my Nordic wife and children; Italy and Greece too far. Somewhere nice and quiet, safe, somewhere we could be on our own, hot and isolated, and cheap to live.

I had never been on a conventional break with my kids, I didn't know where families went. I had always travelled as a single man. Bachelor haunts you didn't take children to. I mentally travelled the same routes I had taken as a youth, re-lived some of the memories, shuddered and threw them away.

'I'm not taking my kids to any of those places!' I thought.

I knew it was hopeless. I couldn't sit here and work it out, not in this dark hole. I had been feeling wretched. It was becoming an obsession, the need to escape a life that sped and raced away too fast to enjoy. I thought of just packing up and seeing where the car led me; then I thought of the wife's reaction and shook my head.

Another summer was disappearing; I felt hopeless when the radio told me the football pre-season games had started.

And I hadn't seen a test match.

Again.

It was Saturday again. Work started to pour through the curtain. I put my head over my hands and made them earn money by obeying my furious demands. No food, just mugs of tea banged on the work bench by Sharon. The radio talked about football, I worked, listened and longed for the day to end, counting my takings every hour the only highlight.

The football results over. Work would slow down. Perhaps I could make an early escape?

The phone rang. I put my tools down, dug into a pile of debris that once had a use, picked up the receiver and put it to my ear. I pushed my shoulder up to hold the phone, then carried on working whilst listening to the Mrs.

"I met Margaret today; her and Finbar are going on holiday next week."

My darling was sprinkling a conversational minefield in front of me.

"Have you heard from your dad lately?" I said hopefully

"They have *three* holidays *every* year," she said in awe

"Good for them," I said sarcastically.

A mistake:

"*We* never have holidays!"

"You do!" I said, knowing I had sprung the trap

As I rarely had a holiday, my wife travelled with the kids alone. She went to see her parents in Sweden, and travelled with my family when they went abroad. Last year she spent three months away. I started to feel single again.

"*You* went to France last year," she said, waiving the bait

"Only to look at houses!"

"And the inside of a hundred wine bottles!"

The phone clicked and went dead.

I dropped my shoulder, caught the receiver, put the phone back on the hook, stood up, danced around the workshop waving my hands above my head, grinning stupidly and silently cheering my head off.

Sat down puffing.

Sometimes, realising how stupid you are is a great relief.

The last time I travelled out of the country.

The last time I had been abroad!

It was that excursion with my fat friend.

'What a div not to have thought of it sooner! Perhaps the free flowing vino helped me forget!'

It was hot, quiet, calm, cheap and easy to get to.

Its perfect!

Last year, my fat friend had phoned and invited me to go to the South of France for a few days.

"I've made an offer on an old house out there; it's been accepted. I have to go and sign, then pay for it. The signing will only take a few hours, afterwards we can look around the area. Do you want to come?" he said

"Yeah, alright mate!"

As I hadn't had a day off work for three years, I reckoned I deserved a few days' holiday.

Fuck the repairs.

The South of France! I had been there once before, to Monte Carlo and Nice. I went with three mates; we had a riot.

"When?"

"Day after tomorrow,"

"Get the tickets, I'll be there!"

My fat friend worked in the fashion industry. He had plenty of work, so I reckoned he was doing OK. He lived in a big house in north London, had a wife and new baby. His wife was a pretty girl who shouldn't have married him. He drank like a fish. He could spin the cap off a bottle of whiskey, pour himself a drink, then spin it back on without you noticing.

He was also as tight as a duck's arse.

In the next few days I made arrangements with my first boss to keep my business ticking over by registered post.

"Holidays in the South of France? What's wrong with Bournemouth?" his only criticism.

We arrived at the airport late, on account of my friend wanting one last drink in the pub.

"A couple more and I'll pay for a cab to the airport," he lied.

We checked-in, then rushed through the airport whilst he argued with somebody behind him.

"Come on! We'll miss the fucking plane!" I said.

He just grinned. He travelled a great deal so knew the rules.

I guess that's how we ended up sitting in first-class with second-class tickets, drinking good whiskey.

Free.

"Where does this plane land?"

"At Toulouse."

"How long will it take from there?" I asked, not knowing where Toulouse was

"I've got a hire car waiting, it won't take long!"

By the time we had the hire car on the road, the effect of all that free whiskey was making it difficult for my friend to drive. It was a great relief to get him, myself and the car off the motorway in one piece.

Then we were gliding through the French countryside.

We had been driving for over an hour. I hadn't seen a car or a house for the last fifteen minutes, so I said:

"This isn't much like the South of France I remember!"

"It's more the south west really," said Tom with a sideways glance I had seen before and didn't trust.

Grabbing the map off his lap, I tried to find Toulouse.

My finger strayed further and further from Monte Carlo. Until finally, I said in frustration:

"Where the *fuck* are we?"

"Take your finger over to the Spanish border, on the Mediterranean side, then come in a bit," he said, looking straight in front of him.

Eventually my finger found where we were going.

"There's nothing here! We're going to the middle of fucking nowhere!" I said, shaking the map at him

"You'll love it!" he said, laughing his fat belly off.

And I did.

Eventually.

The wild beauty of the area became a stronger pull than Tom could manage on the wine bottle's cork. The place was hot, with endless acres of rolling green hills that eventually got higher and higher to become the Pyrenees.

During our few days' holiday, we visited the med several times. We drove through hot, sandy villages dotting the coast line, in the morning, then up to the cool mountains after mid-day.

I had never been anywhere so remote and beautiful.

From the seashore, I could see the snow on the mountain peaks. Hundred of miles of open, uninhabited, Mediterranean wilderness.

In between the sea and the Pyrenees, an unbarred sky.

Air that didn't smell of kebab and fish'n'chips.

I thought my friend better company without his wife. He thought me better company than his wife; I didn't nag about his drinking, though at times I wondered if he had hollow legs. We stopped at least three times during each outing to test the local wine and aperitifs .

We both preferred the small village bistros and bars. We ate paëlla in a village near the Spanish border and washed it down with bottles of cold La Clape. We ate bowls of Cassoulet in the mountains and helped our digestion with delicious Corbières.

Every night we stopped at any village that's bunting suggested a festival, then spent the night revelling, not understanding a word of people's conversations, and not caring.

Anonymous drunken fun.

We wasted little time sleeping because Tom was an insomniac. We were always on the road by eight o'clock each morning, heading towards another dusty village and another highly recommended restaurant. We were never short of conversation; that was one of the reasons why we were friends. Although we had few shared interests, one exception was the ability to drink a lot and be merry. We both liked a tipple, but few men could consume alcohol like Tom.

"When do you ever get it together with your Mrs? You're always so pissed!" I asked him one night as we were getting dressed to go out

"We don't have a problem with that: I don't like it and she doesn't believe in it!"

'Bollocks!' I thought, 'That's what she tells you!'

After one long, hot, glorious day, we stopped at a village called Mirepoix. The local people had decorated the centre square and were all dressed up in crusader's attire. There was obviously going to be a festival.

At the first café we saw, Tom commandeered a big round table that had several chairs pushed under its top; we pulled two out and settled down to watch the parades. Spectators were gathering and forming groups outside the cafés strategically separated around the ill-preserved, medieval square. They covered the pavement and most of the road. We had found a spot where Tom could see the waiter and I could see the talent.

For Tom, the first drinks of the night were always three very large whiskeys; I always started with a beer. We prattled, laughed and gulped. The passing parades started to saunter by; they didn't disturb our supping. The only real movement either of us made was Tom's arm going up in the air to order wine. After Tom had raised his arm several times, we gave up ordering one bottle at a time and started to order two.

The night was fair; the cold white wine disappeared at a steady pace. We laughed and talked of nothing serious. The crowd was beginning to press against our table. Seating was at a premium. A young man with his good-looking girlfriend indicated a chair; Tom nodded his head and waved his hand, so ten of them sat down, boy- and girlfriends.

The youngsters were drinking heavily and one boy in particular was beginning to look and sound very pissed. After several more bottles of white wine, one of the prettier girls at our table staggered down to our end and asked for a cigarette. As we had been a happy group, and as Tom was trying to attract the waiter's attention, I gave her an unopened packet of his. Tom leant back in his seat, which was of the white, modern, bendy, plastic variety, and not best suited to his fat arse. This time it collapsed. The youngsters laughed and giggled. The waiter appeared from nowhere and heaved my friend back into his seat before he could give any more people a laugh. He then turned on the youngsters and though I didn't understand a word he was saying, from the tone of his voice, the stabbing of his finger and the fire in his eyes, I could tell they were being told to fucking shut up and mind their own business.

As a reward for this waiting excellence, my friend ordered three bottles of wine, then gave the waiter one.

After midnight, the crowd started to dilute, the festival was ending. Tom was whispering a very long, complicated story about a white couple and a black baby in my ear. The young man who was pissed at nine o'clock was now paralytic and started to shout. The aggression in his voice attracted my attention. As I looked towards his end of the table, he said something to the pretty girl sitting on his right then sat motionless gawping at her and listening to her answer. Whatever she said, he didn't like. I watched him bring his hand back across his chest, then viciously swing the back of it into her face; as she fell over backwards, I could see blood flowing from her nose and mouth, and a black gap appear where her front teeth used to be. The youngsters around our table were frozen to their chairs and the people sitting at surrounding tables were rewinding their mental videos in disbelief. My body became very hot and that vein in my forehead thumped. I stood up, then looked at Tom; he was scanning the scene. He felt my eyes on him, then turned his bearded head towards me.

"Rob*ert*!" he mouthed, shaking his beard.

He sounded just like his wife.

"Fuck off!" I answered.

It took two steps to get to the other side of the table, by which time the drunken boy was looking up at me with his hands gripping the arms of his chair; I lurched at him, grabbed the collar of his bomber jacket, pulled him up and twisted him round at the same time, swinging him against one of the wooden pillars that held up the canopied roof we sat under. I pulled him towards me, then butted him. Blood spurted from his forehead. I meant to get his nose for a soft landing but missed. The pain made me angry so I thought I'd do it again, only this time properly. At that moment his body became heavy and limp, I let him slip from my grip. He fell back into his chair. I heard a scuffling sound behind me, then felt two arms come over my shoulder. At the same time my legs were kicked from under me. I saw the ceiling, then the front door of the café as the back of my head hit the floor. I felt the pressure of a body on my stomach and my head being forcefully kept down. Opening my eyes and looking up, I saw the round black hole of a gun barrel looking down at me. Above the gun, one copper's face was screaming hysterically. Behind him sat the boy I'd butted. He wasn't being restrained; he sat calmly on his seat, holding a napkin to his bloody forehead as if nothing unusual had happened. I was to find out another day that the boy was a local policeman's son.

The waiter appeared to save me from incarceration. He was shrieking louder than the two coppers, and pointing at the injured girl who had been helped back up off the floor, her nose and mouth still pouring with blood. It was obvious that these weren't the sharpest policemen in the world; the information being shouted at them by the waiter was taking far too long to sink in and the gun was still being shoved in my face. The boy remained seated, not saying a word but glaring hatefully at me. The two pigs still hadn't seen the girl and her now disfigured face, so in desperation the waiter leapt across my body, between the two policemen, grabbed the girl by her arm and swung her round to face the coppers. The other diners gasped in horror and the two pigs stopped, dumbstruck.

Eventually the gun was lifted away from my face and the policeman with his knee in my chest stood up.

The one who'd been holding my head down by the hair had gone over to the young lady, no doubt to get a first-hand version of how she got smacked on the nose.

By the time I stood up, the coppers had decided that the best thing to do was ignore me.

I walked back towards Tom and sat in my chair, rubbing the back of my throbbing head.

My fat friend's belly wobbled with laughter,

"Won't you ever learn?" he grinned at me

"Bollocks!" was my witty reply.

The waiter reappeared with a tray carrying two huge glasses, both half-filled with brandy. After a while, the youngsters and the policemen disappeared. We finished our brandy. Then I said:

"Come on, let's get back to our gaff!"

Tom drove home as if he hadn't had a drink.

I kept one eye closed.

My head ached.

We arrived back at the small house we were staying in. Tom opened the door, put the light on, then walked in.

I followed.

Half-way across the living room rug, a loud husky cough from outside the open door turned me around. Standing in the doorway was a middle-aged, scruffily-dressed man pointing a tray towards me that was carrying three frost-covered bottles of white wine. He announced in a loud, English, colonial, baritone voice:

"I've been waiting for you. Let me introduce myself:

Major Jonathon Reynolds. I live three doors up the road, I've a wife and two sons."

The man walking through the open door had obviously known better days; neither his accent nor name went with his clothes. As Tom's jaw had dropped to the floor in astonishment, and I was still thirsty, I stepped forwards, took the tray from the Major, and said:

"Come in then, Major Reynolds."

I walked towards two huge tatty sofas separated by a long thin coffee table, put the tray down on the table and waved the Major towards one of the sofas; from the way he walked, I fancied he'd drunk as much as we had. The big giveaways were his odd shoes and back-to-front jumper.

"Only down here for a while. The wife suffers from a nervous disorder," he explained, feigning concern.

After several glasses of wine, we deduced they'd been living here for several years, scraping by anyway they could. After a few more drinks, we learned about his Etonian background and the man his parents paid just to change his ski boots.

He then told us about his major financial crisis:

"I go to the bank, I give them a cheque and they won't give me any money! I can't understand these French banks!" he said

"Did you check the balance first, Major?" Tom interjected

"In England they just gave me the money! Mummy and Daddy looked after everything," he replied.

He looked at the window and crossed his legs.

"Daddy's fault," he continued distractedly, "no head for business. The small pension we receive from the trust hardly keeps us in Beaujolais these days.... Where are you chaps from?"

Tom immediately assumed the accent and body language of his public school; the Major crossed his arms, uncrossed his legs, leant forwards keenly then nodded at Tom's cleverness.

Their conversation turned towards cronies they should both have known, but of course didn't. As the Major had been out of circulation for a long time, and Tom had never actually been in it, all they could do was drop unknown names.

Eventually, during a soft silence, the Major turned to me and said:

"And You? What part of the world are you from?"

I wasn't going to say Chelsea; he would get the wrong idea.

"Peckham," I said, being reasonably sure he'd never been south of the Thames in his life

"Where's that?" he asked

"It's near Guacamole," I said then looked at Tom who giggled

"Yes, I think I've been there! I'm sure I was there! During the war" said the Major staring up at the ceiling inquisitively

"Bit of a sticky situation was it, Major?" I said

"Bomb disposal, old son!" he said and tapped the side of his nose

"He's from Chelsea, Major!" Tom snapped irritably

"West ham? Wonderful football team!" the Major exclaimed, trying to sound knowledgeable

"I thought you'd be more of a rugger man, Major?"

"Ah, true old son. The three lions are metaphorically emblazoned on my heart," he said, starting to massage his thighs and stick his chest out as if he'd played scrum half for the lions.

He then changed the subject:

"You chaps should move down here, you know. The area needs people like you to liven it up. Go into property, it's on the up; you'd make a fortune. I'd even let you employ me!"

I was beginning to doubt he'd ever been in the army so I asked him if he'd ever been on the stage.

"Physically, no. But it's my spiritual home," he mused.

Tom started to warm to this conversation and asked the Major what his favourite piece of theatrical dialog was. This was all the prompting the Major needed; he rose unsteadily from the dusty sofa, his wobbly steps taking him past the coffee table and into the only space he considered big enough to perform his forgotten monologue. With his deep, booming voice, he started reciting his soliloquy. Unfortunately, through a mixture of memory loss and acute dipsomania, his voice kept fading away as he forgot the next word or phrase. It came back strongly as he remembered passages that had no relation to what he'd previously been saying. Then it would rise to a crescendo as he got into the flow of nonsensical sentences. His eyes closed during these moments of excitement; we moved further away to avoid the spittle that sprang from between his flapping lips.

The last few bottles of wine were catching up with him; his voice began to dwindle until finally he was silent. His eyes opened and he blinked heavily; I hoped he hadn't seen our chuckling. We clapped and cheered. The Major bluffed his shyness, then wobbled back to the sofa to sit next to Tom. I opened another bottle of wine to toast his fine performance.

Major Reynolds, who by the evening's end had become Major General Reynolds, eventually left us to go back to his wife, who seemingly had given birth to twins in the last hour because now the Major was talking about his four sons.

During the shaking of goodbye hands, we struck a drunken agreement to go into French real estate together and arranged to meet as soon as poss to find ourselves an office.

The Major became tearful.

I didn't know why.

Tom's beaming smile meant the Major was here to stay.

I immediately staggered up the stairs, into my room and fell onto my bed. Just before passing out, I heard Tom open the drinks' cabinet; there was a clink of glass as a bottle was lifted up, then the spinning of a cap.

'How does he do it?' I thought, then fell asleep.

The following day, Tom was propped up in a big leather armchair on a tiny wooden-decked terrace; he was barbecuing the estate agent. The four of us (me, Tom, the estate agent and her effeminate hippy husband) sat round a shabby plastic table. Tom's cheque book was sleeping on the table in front of him. Each day we'd been here, he had phoned the agent and lied:

"Be over this evening for the signing!"

It was now our last night here.

He was still keeping them waiting.

The agent's eyes brushed across the cheque book every time Tom leant forward to refill his glass with their Andorran whiskey; the bottle nearly empty, Tom started to survey the terrace for another one. I was keen to put in an appearance at one more festival, so leant forward, picked up his cheque book, opened it and said:

"*Sign it*!"

The agent slumped with relief, her husband stood up to fetch another bottle; I waved him back down and tried to make Tom fill the cheque in properly, goading him into handing it over. He slowly teased the cheque out of its book, folded it in half and pushed it under his glass. I stood up, shook those poor people's hands and pushed fatty off their terrace, through their house and to the car. I opened the passenger's door, plonked him in, huffed around to the other side, got in and drove off.

Tom was grinning like a happy dog.

"What's funny?" I said dreading his answer

"I put the wrong year on that cheque," he said, squinting at me from the sides of his eyes and sighing innocently, "oh never mind then! I'll post them another one from England!"

I crunched the gears and laughed.

That evening, Carcassonne was packed. We staggered from café to bar, watching the bright costumes saunter by. I looked at Tom's face, thinking perhaps this is one piss-up too many, so said:

"This is the last drink mate!"

He was too wasted to answer.

Eventually, I drove us home in silence. There would be no spinning tops that night, just a sudden rusty grating of bedsprings followed by salivated snoring.

The following morning, Tom's insomnia didn't bother him. His alcoholic energy had run out; I couldn't get him out of bed. Our flight wasn't until 8 that evening, so I emptied his trouser pockets of money and keys, and took the car. I wanted another look around the mountains.

It was good to be alone.

I stopped at a supermarket and bought myself some food, got back in the car and drove along half-hidden country tracks until I was lost in the numerous hills that precede the Pyrenees. I stopped the car by a river which flowed alongside a field crammed with row after row of brilliant sunflowers, their heavy yellow heads filling the air with a dusty perfume. A cascade of light green willow trees decorated the banks and the hot sun's dappled light reflected off the clear water.

I got out of the car and took the plastic shopping bags to the edge of the water. The grass was a soft luminous green, spot-lighted by the sun, so I sat down, unpacked the peaches, pâté, olives, soft cheese and long bread, spread them out and began to eat. I ate the food, dropping bits of bread and watching the river take them away.

I only managed two glasses of wine.

I was woken by a strong cool breeze. I opened my eyes, stared up at the clear-blue sunny sky and realised:

'I don't want to go back to fucking Peckham.'

That evening we flew home, both of us excited, not caring why.

'Yes, that's the place to go! It's perfect!' I thought, 'Very isolated. But that would only be good for me. Nobody there, no stress. I'll work in the sun, plant vegetables and watch them and the kids grow. Should have enough money to live there for a year. Then the good times will be back. A year to rest, recover, then return bronzed, bilingual and ready to start again."

A great plan.

But what was that place called? I couldn't remember.

I walked up the steps, through the mouldy curtain and into the shop to ask Sharon if she had kept that picture of France I'd given her after getting back from my pissed-up jaunt with Tom. She'd asked me to send her a card; I nicked her a postcard Tom had bought for his wife.

"I pinned it te de shewlf inna kitchen," she said.

I walked through the other mouldy curtain into the kitchen. The card was still there. I unpinned it and looked at the picture on the front; the name of the region was printed in bulbous red letters across the top. Put it in my back pocket, stepped back through the curtain and grinned at Sharon.

"Find it did ya?" she said

"No," I lied.

Tried to work, but my head was in a hot part of France. I tried to make the jewellery repair itself; it only twisted into a knotted mess. I threw my overworked tools at the wall, then took my nerves to the curtain, put my coat on and walked out.

The fat, smelly Doorman was stood there grinning at me. He had been nicking my repair money for years, then lost it on shuffling racehorses.

I detested him

"Leaving early ain't yer?"

Normally I would have made an excuse as he reported all my movements back to the new owners.

"Open the fucking door" I said and stared back into his watery, yellow eyes.

He pressed the buzzers. I walked out.

## CHAPTER TWO

Persuading the wife to pack up and leave her beloved Chelsea was definitely going to be a major problem.

The way to go about it, I thought, was to say the house would be on a short term let.

Never use the word 'emigrate'. Say holiday.

Emphasise the benefits to the children: speaking two languages, fresh air, healthy living, sunshine, swimming in the clear lakes, walking in the mountains, eating food grown in a vegetable patch, endless clear blue sea to swim in, a holiday for a whole year.

How could she resist?

Easy!

"No," she said.

"No! We have spent four and a half years rebuilding this house, I have just got swept out the last of the dust and for the first time I'm enjoying living here. I love my life in Chelsea, so *you* think of something else!"

I didn't have to: my eldest daughter's ears came to the rescue. Her teacher at the local Montessori school had said to the wife:

"Your daughter has a hearing problem."

She was right.

Our doctor had given my daughter a hearing test. As I hadn't gone back to work that week, all three of us were sitting in his waiting room, watching a little light above his door, waiting for it to change colour so we could go in.

Once inside, me and the wife could hear the results while my daughter lip read.

"Your daughter needs grummets," the doctor said.

He explained that was plastic tubes pushed through her eardrums.

I glanced across at the wife; her face had turned ashen and she was glaring at the poor doctor. She picked her handbag off his desk, stood up, nodded at him, then we both followed her outside.

In the reception, I asked the wife and daughter to wait a minute and popped back into his surgery.

"It's only me!" I said, "Took your advice and stopped work."

"I told you to slow down, not stop!" he said, "What are you going to do?"

He looked worried, so I told him I was going abroad to lie in the sun for a year and get well again. He stood up, shook my hand, and said:

"Robert, if you need any help, phone me. Wherever you are!"

"Thanks," I said and walked out.

A few years later, in a blind screaming panic, I did need his help.

He didn't let me down.

I caught up to the wife galloping down the King's Road, she had my daughter by the hand and was clutching her handbag close to her bosom. We all marched in silence.

It wasn't until we were half way down our street that she spoke.

"Right then," she announced.

We waited for her statement.

"We go to your little French village for one year. It's the car fumes in London that's the problem, not my daughter's ears!"

She took the front door keys out of her handbag, walked up the steps to our house, opened the front door and pranced in, Victoria following her lamely and me, hopefully. She walked into the living room and plonked her handbag on the table. As she turned to walk into the kitchen, she threw over her shoulder:

"Where *exactly* is it?"

I followed her into the kitchen and took out that stolen post card from my back pocket. I stood holding it out in front of me gripping it in both hands, watching her whilst she plugged the kettle in to make a cup of tea. She turned around, smirked at my lame expression and almost snatched the image out of my pleading hands.

She read out loud the words printed across the top:
"THE AUDE!"

She looked at the small coloured pictures and said in a quiet happy voice:

"It's very pretty."

I left her looking at the photos, walked back into the living room, then, when I knew she couldn't see me, punched the air and screamed silently:

"YES!"

After that, there was never a moment's hesitation or doubt. We were going to France. It felt like we were being pulled rather than pushed; everything became so easy.

Got in contact with the estate agent Tom had introduced me to in France, as I knew she had properties to rent on her books

"Yes, I know of houses to let," she said with a suspicious tone

"I want it long term," I said, "at least a year."

"They all say that!" she said, "It's very isolated here. When do you want it from?"

"The first of next month," I said hopefully

"No problem!" she said knowingly.

I asked her if she had the new cheque from Tom

"Yes, with the wrong amount written on it this time," she answered with resignation.

I phoned a London letting agent and asked her if she would put our house on her books.

"I will have to view the house first," she said with nine plums in her throat, "can I come round this afternoon at three?"

"I shall be waiting with a pot of hot coffee and biscuits!" I replied, trying to sound worldly.

A tall, well dressed, beautiful and extremely elegant Sloane Ranger arrived promptly on my front step. She shook my hand lightly, then informed me she would start at the top of the house and I had no need to follow her around, thank you. She bubbled from room to room, taking copious notes attached to a huge clip board. I sat in the living room stirring coffee.

She wafted past and settled down next to me on the sofa, showering me with Chanel No5. Her jewellery tinkled as she bounced around, making me laugh and feel confidant she could have the place let in a trice.

She left as promptly as she arrived; I was left with a spinning head.

She never touched the coffee.

As the jewellery workshop had been very lucrative, it didn't take very long to find a jewellery repair man to take it over.

We arranged to meet at the workshop.

I showed him around, then introduced him to the girls and the shop manager who were all delighted. They made him cups of tea and fussed around him like they had never done with me, but then he was twenty one and I was thirty-nine. The manager seemed to salivate.

I took the new man into the workshop to instruct him in the practicalities of the repair delivery service.

I asked him what sort of car he had.

He told me.

I told him to get a faster one.

He asked me why.

"To go faster," I said

"What do I wonna go faster for?"

"To stay in front," I answered, then gave him a list of the other shops he would be working for and the directions and times he had to be there.

"I'm not fucking superman," he said lazily

"Do you want this business or not?"

"Yeah of course I do, it's good money!"

"Then are you gonna do what I say?" I said and stared down at him, not wanting him to let my old customers down, "'Cos if you're not, get out now!" I barked

"Yeah, yeah! I can do it. I'll be back on Friday!"

"No you won't, you'll come here when I tell you, now get out!"

He sounded tough enough to survive. I didn't take any money off him as I reckoned he would need all he had. I told him he could move in the day after I had left and not before.

After he left, I stomped around feeling angry. This place may be a shit-pit crawling with arseholes, but he's getting the business for nothing; I thought he should've shown more respect.

The following week, I officially left the house of horrors forever. I packed up my tools and machines, and collected the repair money the shop manager had kept away from the thieving fat Doorman. As I was packing up, some of the girls and the manager came into the workshop with tea and cakes to say goodbye. The girls gave me cards and kisses.

Sharon stayed upstairs behind the counter:

"I'wl keep an nie on de shop," she said solemnly, her drooping eyelids saying something else.

The manager presented me with a pair of engraved cufflinks.

He wanted to make a small speech, he said, so we all sat down on the wooden chairs the girls had brought into the workshop. His new boy sat down and crossed his legs, entwining one around another. He folded his arms, pursed his lips and turned his head to face the wall; the little darling didn't like someone else getting the attention. The manager stood up, we all tried to look attentive.

"Robert is leaving us, after we have been through so much together; the robberies, the staff," he said looking at the newest rent boy, "we have spent a lot if time in each others' company, and Robert's always been there."

His eyes started to glaze over, his tobacco-coated voice faltered. He wiped his eyes, straightened up and continued whilst his boyfriend fidgeted.

"We won't miss him! I'm just happy he's getting away from all this shit." He whimpered and waved his arms around.

His voice started to tremble. A big white hanky appeared from his trouser pocket to cover his entire face. He blew his nose and started to talk again, but this time the tears flew out of his eyes. He turned sharply, ran up the workshop stairs and through the curtain.

"Silly cow!" said the latest piece of prime beef, who stood up and went after him.

The girls looked sad. I stood up and walked over to my overcoat that hung on a hook attached to the far wall. I reached in to the inside pocket, taking out six small, pink coloured, oblong packages. Walked back over to the girls and dropped one into each of their laps.

"Open them when I've gone," I said and poured the tea out.

The girls picked their cups up and sipped. I went back up to the shop, went into the kitchen and waved the prime beef out. The manager sat at the small table, smoking; his nicotine-covered fingers trembled. I sat down next to him and put my hand on his arm.

"I'll be back in a year. Perhaps by then we could get a shop together?" I said

"I'll never see you again, and good riddance!" he answered and stared at the wall.

I put my hand in my trouser pocket, took out a leather box then gave it to him. He opened it and gasped at the sight of a gold pen.

"Now write that fucking book you've been promising for the last four years, you old poof!" I said, walking out of the kitchen and back through that curtain whilst ignoring the fat smirking Doorman.

Tea over, cups cleared, I finished loading my car with the remainder of my tools.

Went back down into the empty workshop one last time. I stood wondering how I had managed to work for so long in this stinking dungeon.

I felt a small breeze, turned and saw Sharon standing in the gap between the curtain and the wall. I looked up at her, surprised she was there. The hair that changed colour every week now looked like a purple brillo pad flattened to the top of her head; the normal self-confident swagger was exchanged for a limp looking lily.

"Can I come in?" she asked for the first time, ever.

I just nodded.

She walked down the stairs slowly and said:

"You're going then? To France?"
She looked at the floor
"As soon as I get out of here," I said quietly.
She walked towards me, stopped and dropped her head again
"What's the matter?" I said quietly
"Take me with you!"

"Take me with you; *please take me with you*! I could look after the children, wash, clean, *anything*! I have some money, you wouldn't have to pay me, I could help your wife!"

Months before, having noticed the occasional bruises and scratches on different parts of Sharon, I privately asked one of the ravens about them:
"Its 'er old man, a barstad he is. Drinks, gambles, never works. And she gets the Saturday night good idin'."
Now the idea of a free cleaning lady appealed to me, but I knew the wife wouldn't have it; the home was her domain and no other woman would ever get in.

"I'm sorry love, I can't."
Pulled her towards me and gave her a cuddle. She sighed deeply.
"I knew there wasn't much chance, but never mind!" she said lying against me.
We stood like that until there was a cough from behind the curtain.

She shook herself backwards pulled at the ends of the tepee she was wearing as if to straighten the pattern out and said:

"Enywaey, me? I got loads to do. I'm gonna open a shop in Cheelsea and sewl home made candawls to dem posh peopwle!"

She reached up on tip toe, kissed me, reached down took my hand, squeezed it, then ran up the stairs and through the curtain.

The suited slimeballs heard I was leaving today, so they had made themselves scarce. For the last time, I walked up the steps and through that shitty, mouldy curtain. Walked round the counter, past the Doorman, silently thanking God I'd never have to smell him again, stepped in the middle of the shop's floor, stopped, turned round, held my arms up above my head and bowed to all the assistants perched around the counter. Turned and walked out of the door to a chorus of:

"Tat tar luv!"
"Don't do anything I wouldn't do!"
"See ya!"
"Keep yer 'and on yer 'apenny."

Driving back to Chelsea, *'Please, take me with you'* dug into my head.

'That makes two more jobs,' I thought.

When I got home, the wife was scrubbing and cleaning. She turned her head towards me when she heard me come through the front door, dropped a scrubbing brush into a plastic bucket and said:

"That letting agent has been on the phone. She's bringing around three Dutch men at nine o'clock tomorrow to see the house."

The wife had gotten to work immediately. Already she had stored in the loft what she didn't want to take and packed what she wanted in the dining room. I was stood in the dining room at that moment.

"You do realise there's four of us and a Maestro? Where are you going to put this lot?" I said to a wiggling bum

"That's your problem!" came the unanswerable reply.

Tow bar and trailer: that's what I need! Never had one before so wasn't sure what I was buying. Dragged out the yellow pages, found the shop I was looking for, phoned them and they said:

"Bring the car round. We'll have the tow bar on tonight."

Six o'clock that night it was on the car; a gleaming tow bar, and so it should gleam for that price! I had often wondered what the wife did with all that money she spent. Now I realised: living costs a fortune, and when you're not working, twice as much.

'Still, never mind,' I thought, 'soon be living cheaply in rural France.'

The next morning, the Sloaney letting agent arrived with three young men. They spent half an hour trying to keep up with her as she galloped them around the house. I was staring at our pile of luggage in the dining room; it was getting bigger and bigger. The Sloaney came up behind me and said:

"They're Dutch, you understand?"

She stared at me. Not really understanding at all, I nodded and said:

"My wife's Swedish."

This seemed to be the right thing to say because she grinned and sprinted off again to catch up with her clients.

Ten minutes later I went to the window and saw her marching them out of the house. They followed like a line of chicks. She steered them into her shiny black BMW. As the car pulled away, she looked back and beamed an enormous grin at me.

Our house started to echo; Viv had emptied everything except essential furniture out of all of the rooms and the house felt as if we had gone already. She had scrubbed and cleaned, cleared and swept until everything shone. My eldest daughter, dressed up in cleaning clothes to look like her mum, had been sweeping the same pile of fluff around the living room for hours. I had packed books and paintings into a cupboard in our bedroom, then gone downstairs to the dining room for a cup of tea Viv had made for me, when the phone rang. Viv answered it, nodded her head then handed me the receiver.

The chief slimeball's voice was squeaking down the phone:

"You want to see me?" he said

"Yeah, I've something to tell you that will increase your profits."

"Are you taking the piss?"

"Meet me and find out."

We arranged to meet two hours later in a café on Tooting Bec station.

He was the managing director of the slimeball company. I had phoned his secretary the day before and asked her to tell him to get in touch, soon. I didn't want anything more to do with this lot, but this was one of the two jobs I had left, so I drove across town, parked the car and walked into the station.

By the time I got to the café, he was already sitting at a dirty table by the window. The table in front of him was covered in ash; he was a serious smoker. He looked nervous and out of place.

I knew the reason he had come here was because he thought I knew something about his shit company and was going to try and squeeze him for money

I sat down opposite him and ordered a cup of tea for myself and nothing for him.

"Well? What have you got to ask me?" he said in a hurry and lit another fag from the end of the last one

"I'm not going to ask you anything. I'm going to tell you something. I don't want anything from you; money, favours, nothing!" I said putting my hand over my cup to keep his stinking ash out

"Why would *you* tell *me* anything?"

"Because I don't want you sacking the wrong people. During your next stock take, you're going to get a big shock, and I owe some of the people in that shop."

"Someone's nicking the stock?" he said and slipped to the edge of his seat, interested now.

I knew this bloke, puffing endless fags, was a prick, but he was sharp and as slippery as an eel.

"They're having your trousers down," I said and leant backwards.

He leant further forward until the front of his coat was scraping the ash off the table top.

"Who?" he snapped.

I leant towards him.

"The fat Doorman," I said into his face.

"How?"

"I don't fucking know! Or care! What I do know is he loads up your display window in his flapping pockets every night. He's got it all stashed in a wall safe that's under his kitchen floor."

"How do you know all this?" he asked and started to lean backwards

"Because the geezer he's using as a fence is a mate of mine; he's already done three deals with him."

"How do you know where the Doorman hides it?"

"Because they do the deal in the kitchen, soppy bollocks!" I said and looked pissed off

"Why would the fence tell you?"

"Because he knows I hate the fat git, and he owes me a big favour."

"What's that?"

"Mind your own fucking business, but if you want you gear back you only have two days left. After that the fence will buy it off him and you'll never see it," I said and finished my tea.

The slimeball had gone scarlet. He took another fag out of his old cigarette case, lit it and said:

"That fat barsterd! I trusted him! I gave him a rise, I got him a fucking tax rebate, now I'll get him five years in Brixton!"

He stood up and wiped the ash off his lapels. I stood up, walked past him and left the café. He was making me feel sick.

I walked back to my car and drove back to sanity, thinking:

'One down, one to go.'

The man who fitted the tow bar had given me the address of a firm that sold second hand trailers, and so after the Sloaney left, that's where I went. They had hundreds of them. Picked a small, tidy looking one, snapped it onto my shiny tow bar, paid the man cash and it followed me home.

The wife took one look and said:

"That's not big enough."

Went and bought wood and metal from a DIY store to build the sides up in an effort to gain more space. Even made a lid with a lock.

It was now small and square, but as tall as the car.

The next day the Sloaney phoned:

"They'll take it," she said plumier then ever, "Isle come rind with the contracts for you to sign in an arh."

'This will be an experience,' I thought.

She breezed in, waving a contract at me in triumph. This time I wouldn't let her escape the coffee and biscuits.

"Sit down and have something to drink while I read through the agreement," I said with authority.

She sat down gripping the contract tighter.

"It's all legal jawgon. Standard stauff!"

"*It* may be standard, but you're not," I said grabbing the contract from her.

After reading the contract, I reckoned she ended up with a lot of money and me, not much. Told her what I didn't like. She huffed and puffed, then went away to make the alterations . She was back in an hour, less breezy, more earnest.

"Is *this* what you want?" she said through clenched teeth whilst thrusting the new version of the rental agreement at me.

I read it and said:

"No!"

We spent half an hour wrangling over her enormous commission. Eventually she gave in and halved her percentage. She stood up ready to go.

"If you would like to see the tenants, I'll send them rind," she said

"Just give me their phone number and I will arrange all that," I said.

She thrust her long, red-tipped fingers towards me. I took her soft-skinned hand and looked into those blue lashed eyes. She batted her eyelids, squeezed my hand and said:

"Lucky old France!"

She dropped her hand and her eyelids, turned to leave and swished her hair in front of my face. I watched her well-shaped backside wiggle its way out of the front room, along the hallway, down the front steps and out to her enormous, expensive car. She opened the door, sat on the driver's seat and looked back to check I was still looking at those long stockinged legs which she then placed delicately under the steering wheel. She flashed me the world's biggest smile, put her foot on the accelerator, then purred away.

I laughed.

"What a performance!"

I watched the car disappear.

"That one needs watching; keep *'er* on a tight reign."

I closed the front door softly.

The following day the estate agent from France phoned to say she had found us a pretty little house on a farm. It would be available four weeks after we arrived in France. In the meantime she was going to put us in a gite.

'Great! That gives me three weeks of cricket before we go,' I thought, 'but what's a gite?'

The three weeks disappeared in a flash. I stood in our cricket pavilion watching the colts push the sightscreens away for the last time this season, wondering when I would play cricket again. Went back into the club house bar to finish the night's celebrations off.

I hate goodbyes so didn't mention to anybody I was going away.

The day before we were to leave, my job was to load the trailer and check the car. Cleaned the car, packed, then repacked. Eventually the poor trailer looked as if it wanted to sit down. The wife kept reappearing with 'just a little bit more' so put the lid on, locked it and asked the wife to put the rest in the back of the car. She did, leaving only enough room to squeeze the kids in.

I'd finished by noon.

I unhooked the trailer from the back of the car, went back into the house and told Viv I had one last errand to complete.

"Ill be back in a couple of hours!" I yelled at a bottom hovering the stairs.

I got into the car and drove it towards Peckham.

I reckoned she would still be at work, and he would have finished his hard day at the dole office. Driving back towards South London when I really didn't want to was making me screaming mad. I drove into a grimy council estate and asked a group of people holding up a wall directions. They leaned harder against the wall and ignored me.

I eventually found the small council house by luck; the purple window frames and plastic window box filled with imitation flowers gave it away. I stopped the car against the kerb opposite this house, closed the driver's window and sunk back into my seat. I watched the houses net curtains until I recognised his silhouette moving around the living room. Then I waited until I was sure he was alone.

When I was as certain as I could be, I leaned over the back of my chair and dug out a piece of lead piping I had hidden under the stuff on the back seat that morning. I slid it up my coat sleeve, got out of the car, locked it, walked over to the house I had been watching and rang the bell. The door was opened by a tall, tanned, handsome man dressed in a colourful shirt, jeans and no shoes.

He looked very well scrubbed.

As he opened his mouth to speak, I let the piece of lead pipe slip down into my right hand; his eyes looked down towards the movement. I swung my hand up above his head, then brought the pipe down as hard as I could across his shoulder blade. I picked a spot I could see exposed by his unbuttoned shirt. At the same time as hearing the cracking noise, I saw the pipe sink into the gap between the two broken ends of the smashed bone, then I pulled the pipe away from him. He brought his good hand up and tried to protect the fragmented bone; I had anticipated this, so I lifted the pipe again then brought it down onto the bridge of his nose. He fell backwards.

I watched the blood from his face splatter up against the grotesquely patterned wallpaper.

Before he could start to scream, I knelt down on his chest and dug the pipe into his ear:

"Make one sound, you fucking wanker, and you'll never hear again! I'm going away, but if I hear Sharon's got bruises again, I'll come back, and next time it will be your fucking neck that's broken, do you hear me, arsehole?"

He blinked 'yes'.

I stood up, stepped back, then kicked him in the crutch as hard as I could. He curled into a ball. I put the pipe back up my sleeve and walked out, closing the door behind me.

Crossed the road, unlocked the car, got in and drove back to heaven.

Both jobs done now.

The new tenants turned up to the house for the front door key. They told me they were in London working as architects to design the redevelopment of King's Cross station. I wondered how Dutch men would modernise the old station? Had a vision of windmills and tulips.

My eldest daughter asked them which one was to have her room. The tallest one looked at her and said with understanding beyond his years:

"Nobody. We will keep it as it is until you come back!"

He understood in a flash something I had not even thought about; she didn't want some stranger sleeping in her bed.

As I hated driving I decided to ignore everybody's better judgment and sail from Plymouth to Santander. It meant landing in Spain, then motoring up to France, but it looked the shorter drive.

"Will take twice as long," was the general opinion, but I loved boat trips and this one went across the Bay of Biscay (visions of Spanish galleons and raging storms!).

After three years deep in the bowels of London, I trembled with excitement.

At last! We were off!

The trailer loaded; kids squeezed in; the wife in the passenger seat surrounded with handbags, carrier bags, string bags, paper bags and thermos; we were heading down the motorway.

"Cup of tea, dear?" the wife said after a couple of hours

"Please," I said.

My eyes had spent more time looking in the side mirror during the last hour than on the road ahead. The trailer looked as if it wanted to lean backwards and I was sure there was something hanging off the end. So, while the wife poured the tea out, I pulled into a lay-by.

"Must stretch my legs!" I said as I slid out of the car to steal a look at the trailer, which looked as if the contents had all slipped to the rear and were trying to get out. I opened the lid; nothing inside had moved, it was too tightly packed. Got back into the car, smiled, drank the tea and set off again, my eyes straying to the side view mirror every ten seconds.

At last we arrived in Plymouth. Found the hotel I had booked us into, parked the car in the hotel car park, grabbed our overnight things, checked in and, after negotiating various lifts and staircases, opened the door to our room. It was big and airy with a balcony. Pushed everybody inside then said:

"Just popping downstairs, won't be long!"

I drifted back out of the room. The wife liked me out of the way at times like this. Ran downstairs and out to the car park. The back of the trailer had started to collapse; it nearly touched the ground.

'Take everything out then put the light stuff in the back and the heavy things in the front,' I thought, 'just get on the boat, then worry about it.'

Emptied everything out. Eventually the car and trailer were surrounded by our worldly goods. It was at this stage I heard the wife's voice coming from above me. Looking up, I saw three heads leaning over our balcony, roaring with laughter. My luck! I had checked into the room above the car park. Repacked the trailer and was delighted to see the back of it had gone up three inches.

Returned to our room and lied that I was looking for the maps of Spain.

The wife had everything in order as normal; beds turned up, kids fed, washed and in their pyjamas. I showered, changed, then sat around waiting.

Eventually I crept out of the room and went downstairs into a little jazz bar I had seen on the way in, drank several pints, then staggered back upstairs to bed.

"Get up."

It was the wife's voice.

"It's still dark," I said.

"We have to leave in fifteen minutes to get to the ferry on time, so get up!"

My head felt stiff, heavy and painful. Got up, showered, dressed, then remembered that trailer. The hangover went to my stomach.

Arrived at the ferry in good time. Somehow the wife produced a thermo of hot water and made us all a cup of tea. It was raining and dark. The four of us sat silently looking at all the waiting passengers sitting in their different shaped cars and trailers, wondering where they were all going. The street lamps cast strange shadows over all of us. My eldest daughter looked lonely so started to tell her about the sunshine and the mountains, the sea and the beautiful countryside we were going to. She looked at me, smiled and cuddled up to her mum.

Eventually the ship shimmered and started to come alive. Doors opened, men appeared at their posts, lights came on, all the cars, trailers and caravans woke up and then we were moving forwards, inching closer to those gaping doors and long ramp at the back of the ship.

'The trailer won't like that long bumpy slope,' I thought.

The cars in front of us disappeared into the back of the ship. Then: my turn. Slowed down, inched forwards very carefully. Driving up the ramp, holding my breath, clenching my teeth, squeezing the steering wheel, trying to go over the bumps smoothly, keeping my eyes on the side mirror, watching the trailer: then to my relief we were up and in the ship, everything fine, in line with the other cars and waiting for a man in a big coat with luminous strips down the sides to tell us which way now.

The bottom of the ship looked full to me and just as I was thinking they had overbooked, a huge ramp started to descend from the level above. My heart stopped. The man with the luminous strips was looking at me and pointing upwards towards it. I wound down my window and asked him if he couldn't squeeze me in downstairs. He frowned, shook his head and then nodded it sideways at the ramp. Up I went. I was delighted to find this slope was much smoother than the last one. Then, as the car reached the floor above and went straight, the back of the trailer dipped down and caught the end of the ramp. Loud crunching, ripping noise, followed by a long scraping scream.

"That car behind seems in trouble!" I nonchalantly pointed out to the wife.

Quickly got everybody out of the car and into the corridor that led to our cabin. A quick glimpse at the trailer; I could see some boxes through a piece of coiled up metal.

The cabin was hot and cosy, I just wanted to crawl onto the top bunk and sleep. The wife started to unpack, organising the cabin, then she organised everybody upstairs to the canteen for breakfast. Told the wife to get me anything except doughnuts, then rushed off to find the ship's bursar.

"Show me," he said, so I did.

He looked down at the trailer, put his huge hand on my shoulder and said:

"The ship's carpenter will look after that, don't worry!"

I slumped with relief, gave him a tenner to get the carpenter a drink, then I ran back up the stairs to have breakfast.

Most of the trip was spent on deck, the kids playing under a huge blue sky full of sunshine, the air fresh and salty, the clear green sea disappearing under the boat. It was September, hot and getting hotter as we sped south, my family getting excited about going to live in a place they had never seen. I felt a huge rush of happiness, grabbed the wife and kids, and squeezed them as tightly as I could.

It was that voice again:

"Get up! We're here."

Hadn't slept much. The wife was dressed and ready, the kids were playing in the corridor outside; it was half past five in the morning. This time I leapt out of bed, showered and dressed in minutes, bags packed and down to the car. Jammed everybody in, then, as surreptitiously as I could, wondered around to the back of the trailer to have a look. Relief! The carpenter had riveted the torn metal together again. Only a repair, but it should get us to France.

The huge doors at the back of the ship swung open; brilliant sunlight rushed through the ship, blinding everybody for a second. The wife looked at me and smiled. Down the ramp, out of the doors and into Spain. I followed a line of cars leaving the dock, then out into the streets, smelling the air, feeling the heat, hearing but not understanding a word people were saying, the sudden freedom making me feel light headed.

Followed the signs to Bayonne; all I had to do was turn right there.

Small hitch: the motorway indicated on the map had not been constructed yet. A temporary road had been built so I turned up and on to it. Because it was temporary, I supposed they didn't want to spend too much money on it; the road was more of a dirt track that climbed and descended so steeply that I feared the worst for the carpenters' rivets. After ten minutes of this dusty perilous drive, the wife climbed into the back of the car and she and the kids fell fast asleep. I was grateful for that. I was back to that side mirror, trying to see through the dust, sweating and watching the back of the trailer slowly descend towards the sandy road.

Three hours later we pulled onto the old road to France. I never knew tarmac could feel so smooth! The wife opened her eyes, then opened the map.

"Let's go down to the coast for lunch," she quipped.

We stopped and studied a rugged coastline full of little resorts on the map. Following Viv's instructions, I drove the car off the main road and down a small lane. I had to squeeze round the bends, then negotiate a small dip up the other side of the valley. At the top of this incline the Atlantic Ocean burst into view. I stopped the car. We all jumped out, singing and dancing, feasting our eyes on the beautiful sun-filled sea. After a few minutes, I drove down the coastal road and into a seaside resort that hadn't changed since the fifties. The last forty years had not touched the cafés, hotels or houses. Spanish people sat outside drinking coffee and eating food: pensioners, middle-aged couples, young children, teenagers, brought together by lunch, their brown bodies and laughing faces making us feel warm and welcome.

I pulled up outside a large café packed with people. We must have looked a pitifully tired, frightened sight. The owner and his wife came over to us immediately and asked, mostly in sign language, if we wanted to eat. We nodded greedily. They produced a table, laid it, put chairs out, then waved us onto them. The owner's wife, a big, brown, beautiful, middle-aged lady, produced a bottle of water for the children, two glasses of wine, then disappeared into the kitchen.

"There's no menu," said my tired wife.

We sat sipping the cold, white wine, feeling the hot sun on our faces, hungry but happy. Both the owner and his wife appeared through the kitchen doors at the same time carrying huge trays laden with food. They covered our table with small dishes containing seafood covered in brightly coloured sauces, bread, more water and a bottle of white wine. I thought the children might think the food too spicy. Fifteen minutes later, all the food was gone; the kids licked their lips, their faces and clothes covered in the remains of the coloured sauces. The empty dishes were cleared away and full dishes of ice cream put in their place.

Our first meal on foreign soil had been a great success.

I called for the bill, the total of which wouldn't have paid for the ice cream in London. Everybody full and sleepy, the wife marched us off to the beach. I laid down and went to sleep in on the sand.

SATURDAY

By the early evening we had crossed the Spanish border. One Gendarme gave the trailer a queer look at passport control and a few passing motorist overtook me pointing back over their shoulders with a look of concern on their faces.

Otherwise the drive was smooth and quite.

I turned right at Bayonne and started to drive alongside the French Pyrenees. The kids had hardly said a word although they had been cramped in the car for hours. Viv made us all drinks and bits to eat.

"We will have to find a place to stay the night, a small hotel, if we can find one; our destination is at least five hours away!" Viv was murmering at the map.

We staggered on. The sun disappeared, night time was trying to take over. Both me and Viv were too tired to make a decision where to stop.

We had just drove into a small town that displayed a name board with 'Pau' written on it, when our youngest, who had been strapped into a baby seat for most of the day, let out a screech. I braked; the car stopped and the trailer spun and crashed against the kerb. The impact sounded like a squeezed can popping open. During the loud silence that followed I looked in that worn out side mirror and saw a pair of shoes sticking out the back of the trailer. The wife said:

"That looks like a nice place."

I looked up to see her pointing at a pretty yellow hotel covered in ivy. She got out of the car, unloaded her overnight things, scooped up the children, put her head over her shoulder and told me to park. I dragged the screeching trailer onto the church forecourt opposite the hotel, got out, locked the door of the car, ignored the trailer, crossed the road and went into the hotel. By the time I walked into the lobby, my family had disappeared. I spied a bright, glassy bar with a black handsome barman looking at me. The word 'Bingo' flashed in front of me. I quickly tip-toed across the resplendent yellow carpet, slid through the brassy door and onto a high leather barstool. The barman lifted his eyebrows at me; I pointed at a whiskey bottle, lifted my hands up and drew them a long way apart.

"Do you want something in it?" the dark face said in English

"More whiskey!" I laughed

He made the drink.

"How did you know I was English?" I asked

"The Germans walk in as if they own the place, the French walk in as if they would like to own the place, the English walk in as if they don't give a fuck who owns it!" he said grinning.

"Have a drink on me!" I said in answer.

Before I could order a second one, the wife found me and shuffled me upstairs.

Viv had organised two rooms with a connecting door.

'Bit expensive,' I thought looking around at the posh furnishings and worried about the money we had already spent.

"Although it's late, Madam's going to cook us something to eat," she said proudly.

I nodded, happy the wife could speak a bit of the language; I couldn't understand or speak a word.

The rooms were painted with clear pastel colours, the furniture covered with Laura Ashley upholstery. The girls had their own room, with shower and toilet, a fridge full of Coke and Lemomade, and the peanuts were already eaten.

We all showered, dressed, laughed and giggled, enjoying our good fortune at finding such a pleasant place to stay. I chased the girls around our rooms while Viv did her final fussing. She wasn't comfortable about the girls sleeping in another hotel room, even if there was a door in between which she would keep wide open; her umbilical cord didn't reach across strange bedrooms.

Downstairs, the round table was laid with a huge, bright white tablecloth, patterned serviettes wrapped around shiny silver cutlery, and the centrepiece, a bowl of multi-coloured summer flowers reaching out of a silver vase. Everything was illuminated by six long white candles. There were three armchairs and a high chair for the youngest; even that was decorated with a coloured serviette. Viv opened the huge menu and ordered for all of us. Madam made sure the children were fed and fussed first; she wanted us to have our meal alone not realising the adjoining bedroom door would be kept open. The Menu Enfant was quickly dispatched while I helped a bottle of wine to empty itself. Viv took the kids upstairs to bed. I lit a fag and indicated to Madam that the barman needed me.

After finding out that my new friend was from the West Indies, and just as I had started telling him a brilliant story about Ian Botham, Viv put her head round the door. By the look on her face, I knew this story was too long.

"She's Swedish with a German mother, and Jewish grandparents," I told my black mate.

He opened his eyes wide.

"Run, man! Run!" he said, whilst cleaning a big glass with a white cloth.

The meal consisted of five courses, during which I never said much; I didn't know food could taste so good. We both enjoyed every mouthful, savoured every sip of wine, and when we had finished, floated upstairs to sleep in a trance.

I awoke to a room filled with sunlight. The wife was already pottering about. She had smuggled her electric kettle into the room to make us a PROPER cup of tea. The room had been rearranged the way she wanted it; furniture had been moved, a small table I recognised from the hallway had appeared to serve the tea from, the telly covered over with a small crochet cloth Viv seemed to carry around with her. We would have a quiet cup of tea together and a few digestive biscuits, as we did every morning, no matter where we were.

"Madam has a friend who will look at that trailer for you," the wife said.

A look of panic must have crossed my eyes.

"Stop worrying! There's nothing to do until tomorrow; look out of the window and you'll see why."

I put my cup on the table by the bed, got up and looked out onto a French town during market day. The place was buzzing with people wandering between dozens of display tables, looking at and feeling the local produce.

And in the middle of all this, sat our car and that trailer. One trader had built his display around them and even used the top of the trailer to show off his bunches of lavender. I fell back onto the bed, laughing. Viv poured another cup of tea grinning.

In twenty minutes, my family were scrubbed, dressed and ready to join the market fun. We were all very excited and a little nervous about our first real day in France.

We wandered around in a cultural shock.

Spending all my working days in the slums of South London, this small town with its market stalls, people and peace made me feel safe and secure, even though I didn't understand a word people were saying. These were feelings I hadn't felt in years.

I was happy to let the kids run off and join the throng, the were no threats here. I knew the difference; I didn't feel the pressure of being on guard. The air seemed creamy my feet slowed down and touched the ground lightly. I didn't know why but I wanted to cry.

I was so happy I should have burst.

"Put your bankcard in the machine," Viv demanded

"It won't work here, we're not in England!" I whimpered.

Got one of those stares back, so put the card in, pressed some buttons and money came out.

"You're so continental!" the wife said grinning.

She took the money from my hand and walked away. I stayed thinking:

'That machine just gave me fifty quid, then took it out of my bank account in England? I used to keep it down my sock when I travelled abroad as a youth!'

Deducted fifty quid from what I had left in the bank, shuddered, then went off to do something I had been looking forward to.

Sat outside a French café, drinking coffee, watching country life go by on my own, no hurry, no stress. Just sit and look, think at the pace I wanted to, wander off in day dreams, then come back, sip my coffee and wander off into another.

The market was coming to a peak. The square was packed with people talking, smoking, scrutinising food then buying it, filling shopping bags to overflowing. Depending on which way I turned my nose I could smell either cheese or sausage, fruit or flowers, spices or herbs. Everyone busy, enjoying themselves, the place hummed with expectation.

Lunchtime soon.

The flower seller who had taken over my car and trailer was lifting his shoulders and showing me the palms of his hands. The wife said:

"He's sorry but you're not supposed to park here today."

So I lifted my shoulders and showed him the palms of my hands, and then we both did it again. To make sure he knew that I didn't mind about the trailer, I bought three bunches of his flowers, showed him my palms again and said my first French words:

"Avoir, merci."

My wife and eldest daughter seemed to think this very funny.

"That fifty pound's gone," said the wife, and looked innocent.

I gave the flowers to the lady who ran the hotel. She was obviously an important lady, her clothes looked expensive, her hotel clean and classy; she was good looking and doing well. But this lady didn't take prisoners. I stood next to her as she spoke down the phone to the man given the job of repairing the trailer. After a couple of demanding minutes, she put the phone down, turned and grinned at me. I had not understood a word she'd said, but I knew the trailer would be repaired on time. I grinned back, led her to a display cabinet in the middle of the reception area and pointed to a pair of dress earrings I'd seen the wife gazing at. She took them out, boxed and wrapped them into a piece of pink art, added the cost to our bill, then hid them for me.

Following Madam's directions, I managed to get the trailer to the repairman the next morning. We had to take all our worldly belongings out and put them in the only safe place he had: on the floor of his car showroom.

Driving away, I looked back through his huge, shiny showroom windows. I could see our things piled up the side of a new display car. They didn't increase his chances of making any sales in the next couple of days. To the right of the showroom, I noticed him standing outside his repair shop looking at the upside down trailer and scratching his head. I had a moment's doubt, then I remembered Madam talking to him on the phone.

We had another night in our cosy, fluffy, expensive hotel.

I took the girls out for a walk before bed. We found a small garden at the back of the hotel to play in. After a little while, I decided little girls were no good at football, so sat and watched them invent games using sticks and grass. It was a warm, soft night. I lay down to watch them, listening to their voices, the bird song and the rustling leaves. Shut my eyes and fell fast asleep

Bliss. I dreamt of days to come.

My eldest daughter was whispering in my ear: "Daddy?"

I opened my eyes and looked straight up into Victoria's beautiful face. I kissed her, cuddled her, then cuddled Keira, the youngest, stood up and carried them both back to Mumma.

In the morning, Viv packed. I took our luggage downstairs, then we all drove off to see the trailer repairman.

Another hour, he told the wife.

We had a picnic by the side of a river, then went back again. The trailer was still upside down but only because then he could show us his work: he had rebuilt the suspension! We turned it over; the trailer stood on tiptoe and stuck its chest out. I clipped it back on to the car. Even after loading, it hardly sank an inch. We drove off, the trailer cruising proudly along behind us. I turned to Viv and said:

"He only charged us thirty quid!"

Back at the hotel, gave Madam my credit card then signed the receipt without looking at it.

'That shock can come later,' I thought.

Then we experienced our first French goodbye: shaking hands, kissing, laughing with everybody who worked in the hotel. I gave our address to my new black mate; he promised to drive over and see us when he needed to speak English. All out to the street, more shaking hands and kissing, the girls kissed twice by everybody and told how pretty they were. Finally got everyone in the car, drove ten metres, stopped, jumped out and went back into the hotel. Madam was standing in the middle of the reception holding out that pink box. I took it, then kissed her on both cheeks, then kissed her again, turned round and bounded out to the car; got in, tossed the pink packet to the wife and drove off. While she opened her box, I opened the bill for the hotel. Madam had only charged us for one night and the earrings! The wife had already put them on, her grin stretched from one earring to the other.

"Here's another nice surprise!" I said and gave her the hotel bill.

Being able to travel faster than thirty miles an hour and not having to drive with one eye staring into the side mirror was a luxury. The trailer whizzing behind us, we galloped along. I had phoned the French letting agent from the hotel and explained why we were going to be a day or so late.

"Not to worry, just phone me when you're almost here, then I will give you directions," she said happily.

Five hours after leaving Pau, we arrived in Mirepoix. I phoned the agent, as I estimated from looking at the map we were about fifteen minutes from her house. A child's voice was talking to me down the phone.

"My mummy az gone to a party," he said with a French accent

"Will she be long?" I said desperately.

The phone went clunk as the receiver was put onto something solid. I heard scurrying noises, a banging door, footsteps then;

"Yes, ze party is just starting."

"Where is the party?"

"In Mr 'Arris's house."

"Where's that?"

"Number 13."

"Number 13 what?"

"Number 13 Rue St Jacques."

"Where's that?"

"Next door."

"Can you go next door and ask your mummy to come to the phone?"

The plonk repeated itself. I waited. There were heavier footsteps and the agent answered. She told me she hadn't expected me to arrive so soon. It was too late for the Gite that evening, but we should come to her house and she would sort something out.

That night there were no moon or stars. We blindly followed the road signs and were lucky that they led us directly to the agent's village. Parked the car, then knocked on her door. A little boy answered then guided us to the party.

"Come in, have a drink!" a young English man was saying.

The house was full of Brits in the middle of some sort of celebration.

"We have a big room for you and the children upstairs, plenty of bedding, so relax and enjoy the party!" the agent said.

So that's what we did.

At first a thought the party was fancy dress, a Sixties party, it was only after listening to some of the guest's tales that I realised most of this lot came here on the hippie trail, they had been sitting around smoking pot and drinking cheap wine ever since. They rarely went anywhere and hardly ever had any money, so the records they played and the clothes they wore were the ones they'd brought with them.

We had a great night.

Awoke to the sound of children singing. It was the French version of 'ring-a-ring of roses'. Their voices were coming through our open bedroom window; the clear, hot sky was framed by an old wooden frame set in a creamy plaster wall. My eyes were starting to close again when I realised that one of the voices down there belonged to my daughter. I sat up and looked across at her empty bed, laid back down again and listened. She was out in the village, playing with the local children, singing in French!

The party had gone on until late, so got up, filled a big glass of water, took it over to the wife, nudged her gently and said:

"Listen!"

She drank the water, dragged her eyes open, pushed the sleeping baby away and said through a massive hangover:

"I feel like dying!"

I sat down on the bed and waited.

"Is that our daughter outside?" she eventually said.

We went over to the window, put our heads out and saw a village that looked as if it hadn't been touched for a thousand years. There was a group of children playing outside the church; dark haired, brown, Spanish looking, with a pale-skinned, blond headed one running around with them.

"She's singing 'ring-a-ring of roses' in French!" said the wife.

"That's because we're in France," said I, sprinting into the bathroom.

An hour later we were driving through acres of lavender along undulating hot dusty roads. The few farmhouses we did pass were stone built with tiled, terracotta roofs. The sun was baking the verges and hedgerows brown. We all had shorts and t-shirts on so I made everybody sing 'We're All Going on a Summer Holiday', remembering the picture of Cliff in the shop.

We were following a car driven by the French agent's husband who had been given the job of guiding us. He said he was a builder but looked more like a hippy-poet. They had lived here for fifteen years, struggling to clothe and feed their children, arriving in an old V.W. bus packed with all their possessions. This was the bus I was now following.

I thought about the party the night before. The house was decorated with dilapidated furniture from junk shops, the record player plopping down sounds of the sixties. The guests were dressed in floral jeans, smoking rollups, singing 'We All Live in a Yellow Submarine' through their beards, their long hair hanging off their bald heads. All the women, whether sitting down or standing with a drink in there hand, looked as if they were practicing yoga positions, there kaftans swirling around furiously as they danced to Otis Reading. I started to giggle; 'Talk about trapped in the sixties,' I thought.

The wife said:

"What's funny?"

"Wait 'til this lot hear 'Guns and Roses' and 'The Black Crows'!"

"Just make sure you're not wandering around this place whistling 'Sweet child o' mine' in fifteen years time!" she said whilst changing a nappy.

We had been driving on roads only wide enough for one car for the last half an hour when our guide turned left and we started to go up a steep hill. This carried on past fields of maze and lavender; a big manor house drifted by in the distance; then round a bend, squeezing past a row of farm buildings, down and around, then, up a sharp incline past a field of cows, we turned right. Noticed a cross with Jesus pinned to it standing upright on a stone plinth in the middle of the road. Passed a sign saying. The lane started to go around the village. A small row of derelict houses and a small church appeared on either side. To call it a village was a vast exaggeration. There were only six houses here, half of which were ruins. The poet stopped his hippie wagon and got out making a rollup at the same time. I could feel the wife disapproving beside me.

"This is it," the poet said.

"Where's the rest of the village?"

"This is it," he said again.

"Where's the Gite?"

He pointed to a two-story farmhouse leaning against the church.

"Hope nobody moves the church!" I said.

He rolled up another cigarette and lit it.

We walked through a door with an old floppy sign above it that said 'Mairie' and straight into a rectangular room. There was a small, bird-like woman sat behind a brown desk with a big picture of the French president hung on the wall behind her.

"The village owns the Gite. This is the Mairie's secretary. You pay must her," the poet said.

She stood up and I shook her tiny hand. She sat down and looked at the rental agreement, the president was still staring at me. Gave her the rent money and signed the contract. She gave me the front door key. I shook her hand again, winked at the president and left.

Outside, gave the key to the wife who then drove the car and trailer up to our new home.

The poet rolled another fag and started to walk towards the our new home the Gite. I could hear loud unpacking noises coming from inside and remembering the wife's reaction to the first rollup, steered him towards his van and sent him off with the promise, yes, he would be the first person I would contact if I needed a builder. Then I watched as his van bumped down the hill with him leaning out the window whistling 'Hey Jude'.

## CHAPTER THREE

After the poet left, I walked around the village which consisted of three farm houses that were lived in but closed up, a gap where three houses used to be, then another house that was lived in and open. Opposite that there were two abandoned houses, and next to them the Mairie. As the secretary's car had gone, I lifted the sign above the front door of the Mairie. Underneath written in stone it said 'Ecole'.

There were various bits of building machinery laying around everywhere, and perched above all this, the church and our Gite.

Climbed up the small hill to the church and surveyed the surrounding countryside: miles of soft rolling hills, across the horizon the Pyrenees, not a pylon in sight.

Complete silence, isolation.

'Perfect,' I thought.

I turned and walked towards the Gite. We had a small garden outside our front door where Viv had set up a table and chairs for tea: plates of bread and jam, cake and orange juice for the kids.

"Where's Keira?" I asked

"As she has no high chair, so she's decided to eat under the table from now on,".

"Well this is it, peace and tranquillity!" I said dropping into my chair.

"I wonder where the nearest school is?" said the wife. I looked across at our eldest and saw a look of horror leap onto her face.

"She can't speak French," I bravely pointed out

"She will learn in school, and another thing, what are *you* going to do here?"

I said the first thing that came into my head:

"Property. I think I will go into property."

"There's enough derelict houses here to keep you going for years!"

"I'll get my old flares out, then pop into town and buy some tobacco and roll up papers," shall I

The next morning, someone was tapping at our new front door. As the door was mainly glass, I could see a small man with a very brown, weather-beaten face, dressed in peasant clothes waiting outside with a lady taller than him by his side.. That was the second thing you noticed about him, the first was his great big, curled-up moustache that sat underneath a pair of sparkling blue eyes and on top of a wide grin. He let himself in, followed by his companion . She was plump, very white skinned, with an even bigger smile. This was our first day of rural life.

They gave us soap and sweets, picked the kids up and told them they were beautiful, then took us for a tour of the village. They were the only inhabitants left from a population of 256 in 1963. The Mairie used to be the schoolhouse and the building we were all standing outside, at that very moment used to be the café. Some Germans had started to renovate the inside but had left after their marriage broke up our new friend was telling us as the wife translated. He then took me and Viv aside and started to whisper to us in a dak conspirital tone

" I could get this house very cheaply, you could renovate and move in the village needs children.

We all walked back up to the gite and had coffee in our little garden.
"Ask him his name," I said to the wife.
She did. He said 'Trio'.
"Trio," she said, "everybody calls him Trio."
Coffee over, the 'Trios' left to go to the market.
We followed half an hour later.

I spent the following week giving minor events like shopping great importance, and then rushing off to fulfil these vital tasks. Or sleeping. Victoria spent most of her time running round and round the village catching up with lost exercise, with Keira crawling after her. The wife had transformed the inside of the Gite from a holiday home into her home. Nobody had noticed the absence of a television or telephone, nor would they over the next few years.

The Trios made an appearance most days with gifts and hugs for the kids. A few of the local farmers passed through the village either on foot or aboard a tractor. They were obviously used to 'visitors in the Gite'.

A few days later, the wife said:
"I've seen a small school and have spoken to the head mistress; Victoria can start tomorrow."
She got into bed then turned her light out. I realised this topic was not up for discussion.
The following morning we took our eldest into the local town and dropped her off at her new and very pretty nursery. We sat outside until the clock struck twelve then crept back up to the front door and went inside. There was soft classical music playing and loads of young girl helpers fussing over the children's every need.
Our daughter came up to us neatly packed into her coat
Then from us, the normal, intelligent, adult questions.
"Was it O.K?"
"Did you cry?"
"Are the people nice?"
"Have you eaten?"
"Did you make any friends?"
To which our daughter kissed her minder on both cheeks, glared at us and walked to the door. We shook everybody's hands, said 'merci' too many times and then cowered behind our very brave daughter who was swaggering towards the car.

The great day came. We were to leave the gite and move into the house on the farm. We packed everything roughly into the car and trailer. We knew where to go as we had been passed the place loads of times. Ten minutes after setting out, saw the sign we were looking for:. Took a sharp right along a thin lane perched on top of a steep ridge, then around three more bends, when a small, modern building came into view. Behind that stood a very large, very old farm building. There were two people standing outside the original building, waving to us. I made it half way between the two buildings when the biggest Alsatian I had ever seen bounded out in front of the car. The kids stuck their faces to the window in amazement at the sight of such a huge creature. The dog's bark was deep and loud. I sat rigid in my seat. The wife turned to me and said:

"Get out and say hello to your new landlord."

The new landlord and his wife stood ten yards away, the dog between us.

I hoped they wouldn't let their new tenant be torn to bits, so looked at them with pleading eyes. They stepped forwards and petted the dog, who licked their hands then rubbed himself against their legs. Realising the beast was harmless, I jumped out of the car hoping the wife and kids hadn't noticed my terror. The dog licked my hand and I brushed his fur as if we were old friends. Shook the landlord's then his wife's hand. Over their heads I saw the kids run off towards a barn with the dog. The wife floated past, held her hand out to the landlord, and whispered to me:

"You're my hero!"

I followed the three of them towards the small modern house, looked back and saw Keira lying on her back, giggling whilst being licked from head to toe by that ferocious beast. Looked up and entered the place where we were to spend the next three years of our life.

There were three bedrooms, a kitchen, bathroom and living room, all on one floor. Brown was obviously the in colour when they built this place. Except for the giant fried egg pattern on the wallpaper in the living room and the dark mauve bathroom fittings and tiles, everything was either light or dark brown: a dash of fifties psychedelia mixed with your old aunt's furniture. Not exactly Chelsea.

Viv made the four of us a cup of tea I didn't understand the look of confusion on Mr and Mad face, as I poured milk and ladled suger in to the cup of hot brown liquid. They only took a sip then told us they didn't live on the farm but Mr father did he said , through the wife, he would introduce us to Dad and Mum when they returned that evening. They showed us how the electric fuse box worked, and where to turn the water off.

They were both very considerate and kind, thay tried to be as soft as possible. He was dark and had a Spanish complexion, she taller than him and very fair, he did all the talking, she the smiling.

'I'd better find the kids, give the wife time to calm down,' I thought.

There was a fenced-in vegetable patch between the two houses and this was where I found them, playing with the dog.

"What's that red stain on your dress?" I asked Victoria

"Rabbit's blood!"

She obviously recognised the look of confusion on my face.

"Come, I will show you."

I picked up Keira from the puddle she sat in, wiped the mud from her clothes, then Victoria and the dog led me to the back of the barn. They stopped in front of a gigantic mound of manure.

'What's this got to do with rabbit's blood?' I thought and looked at my daughter inquiringly.

"The dog brought us here. He started to dig into the manure: two baby rabbits ran out and hid under that piece of metal."

She pointed towards a sheet of corrugated iron lying beside an old tractor.

"He became very upset because he couldn't get under it, so I went over and lifted it for him. When the first baby rabbit ran out, he grabbed it and blood squirted out onto my dress."

"And the second one?"

"He just seemed to swallow that one!"

All through this tale of country life, she stood stroking the dog; although he was sitting down he was still four inches taller than her. He seemed to be grinning.

"What's he waiting for now?" I said

"Mummy rabbit to come back."

I carried Keira back towards the house, leaving Victoria with her new friend. As I approached the front door, I could hear the wife clanking pots in the kitchen. Left Keira on the porch, and went in.

"What are the children doing?"
"Playing bunny rabbits."

I went over to the kitchen window and looked out across the vegetable patch which was full and blooming with colour, over a grassy bank. Beyond that was the big farm house and barn full of hay.

The wife came up next to me and said:
"This place is so beautiful."
Then she squeezed my bum.

I left the wife to unpack and took the kids for a walk. We walked up through a wood that sat on the hill above our new house.

"What's that smell?" said Victoria
"Herbs," I said.

We walked down a small rocky slope and sat on an embankment overlooking grass-covered hills. On the horizon we could see the Pyrenean mountains. There were ancient isolated farm buildings separated by irregular shaped fields, some with grazing cows, some full of brilliant coloured sunflowers, others lined with maze, the fruit hanging down ready to be eaten.

Not a cloud in the sky, the sun warm and yellow, we sat down on a rocky ledge covered with rosemary and other sweet smelling herbs I didn't know the names of.

Keira crawled around in the rosemary, eating wild mint, sending up aromatic waves of herbal perfume.

"Smells like mumma's scent here daddy," said Victoria,
rubbing her face into the ground
"A perfume park where the air smells of Viveka!" I said softly. They both turned around.

"Lets pick some mint and take it to mumma," I said, thinking of grummets and car fumes.

The following weeks past in a hazy feeling of strange emotions that were new to all of us. We stayed elevated and excited, everything was new and good, we had come to a place where there was no bad. Regardless how much we waited for it, nothing bad happened. Everything smelled good and looked beautiful. There seemed to be more time in every day, I hadn't worn a watch since the second day we arrived on the farm and had started to look up to tell the time.

Our landlord's father owned the big farm building we could see from our kitchen window. Every morning he went into barn to tend his cows (all five of them) and his wife went into the vegetable patch to pick the fruit and veg for that day's lunch. They fed the geese three times a day. The hunting dogs had to be seen to, the chickens fed and their eggs collected. Madam then sold the eggs in the local market. If there was rain, there were snails to find, then cage and detoxify; Monsieur sold them in the market. Monsieur worked in the vegetable patch to produce the food, Madam the flowers to decorate the house . The weeding, tilling, planting, rotovating, watering and fertilising he did; she fed the weeds to the chickens and guinea foul. Trees to fell, grass to cut for silage, rabbits to shoot, muck spreading, tree planting, ditch clearing, looking after their grand children, never missing a dance or fête, and attending all the local funerals.

Monsieur told us that since his retirement, he didn't have so much to do anymore!

So when I was told to report to the barn on Monday morning to help with the geese, I realised if you had idle hands here, the local people would soon use them.

"What do you think they want me to do?" I asked Viveka,

"I don't know but you have to wear wellies, I've put them by the door."

"Wellies? In a barn?"

"Sounds very messy," she said and shuddered, "still, just remember the muggers and be grateful!"

I put the wellies on and walked towards the barn thinking: 'Whatever they ask me to do, don't be sick.'

Pushed the barn door open, walked in, noticed the geese were not in their normal pen around the back of the dog's enclosure; they had been taken out, put in the corner of the barn and surrounded with bails of hay. I could see their heads poking over the top; they turned their heads sideways and stared at me with one eye. In the barn there were two women I had never seen before, plus Monsieur and Madam. The air was hot and wet with steam coming from a colossal iron pot filled with bubbling water. Immense wooden tables, their tops scrubbed clean, waiting. A cord, with shiny hooks every three feet, stretched across the barn, waiting. I was placed at one of the tables and told to wait. So wait I did. We all did. Then Monsieur nodded at Madam. It was about to begin.

Madam took one of the geese out. She held it by its legs and wings, its head stretched out. Monsieur picked up a stick with a red line painted around the top. He whacked the goose on the head. Madam then hung the unconscious bird by its legs from one of the hooks, then pushed a sharp pointed knife into it's head behind the ear. The blood dripped onto a plate that had bits of bacon and breadcrumbs scattered on it. I could smell the blood, it was sweet and musky. I looked across at the other geese, wondering what they were thinking; their one-eyed stare only showed curiosity.

After several birds had been hung up, the part I dreaded:

My turn.

I had to unhook them, rub a white powder into their feathers, dip them into the hot water, swish them around for a few seconds by their scaly feet, and then lift them onto my wooden table. I was handed a cloth and told to rub the feathers off. To my surprise they all just fell out; I'd always thought you had to pluck feathers. Then one of the ladies took the bird off my table, carried it over to a big bucket of warm water and scrubbed it clean. Then she passed it over a flame coming from a hand burner; this was to make sure all the feathers were gone, including the hard white bits that held the feathers into the skin. She handed it across to the last lady who tied its feet and wings up. They handled the carcasses with exceptional respect.

After about an hour the humid air around my pot stank of damp, dirty feathers, blood and chicken skin. The farmer must have noticed my green face, he moved his wife across to do my job and I was given hers.

I eventually had a go at everything and was just starting to really get into it when the last goose had been prepared.

Madam had disappeared half an hour before to prepare lunch. She was back now, helping all of us to scrub and clean the barn. The geese were all lying on their bellies on the edge of one of the tables, their heads dangling towards the floor.

All of a sudden, there was a nerve-tingling shriek from one of the women. We all looked at her. She was covering her mouth with one hand and with the other jabbing her finger towards the open barn door. Black smoke was belching in. With the nearest fire engine an hour away, the first reaction in isolated places is to put the fire out yourself.

The farmer reacted first. He ran towards the door, moving like a man half his age, me following only just behind him. As I ran passed Madam I noticed she had both hands covering her face. We ran out of the barn into the courtyard, we followed the smoke that led us towards the kitchen; inside the air was black. The boss disappeared into the smoke. I groped around, then found him on the far side of the kitchen. I shouted his name:

"Marcel!"

He turned around, carrying a ball of billowing smoke. I followed him out of the kitchen and into the courtyard. As the air became clearer, the cause of the fire became apparent: a huge frying pan, black and charred and belching. The smoke it produced inside the kitchen was blinding; outside in the courtyard the pan looked small and puny. The farmer threw it against the wall of the barn.

The blood that had dripped from the birds onto the plates of bacon and breadcrumbs had coagulated into a black jelly. Madam had taken one of the plates into the kitchen, plopped the black pudding into the frying pan for lunch, then lit the gas. In her rush to get back to work she left it frying. Madam was a highly respected lady in the local community, which meant the boss would *not* tell her off in public. The other ladies knew this; they huddled around her and scurried her into the kitchen, safe ground there. The boss went back into the barn and threw something else at the wall; I went home for lunch.

After lunch, wandered back down to the farmhouse wishing I could speak some French. Not being able to communicate was like loosing one of your senses. As I approached the farmhouse, the kitchen door opened and Marcel's hand came out; his finger called me in. The kitchen had been cleared and cleaned, the ladies sat around the table knitting. The boss signalled me to sit down and handed me a small glass of coffee. We sat there silent. The ladies clipping knitting needles made me feel even more awkward. I was the one who couldn't speak so *I* had to do something. I stood up and started to mime that morning's adventure, the boss stood up and joined in. Then with body language, French words, cockney English, and clowning, between Marcel and myself we did our best to make two grown men trying to rescue a frying pan look funny. The ladies laughed, so of course we couldn't stop.

Eventually Madam picked up the empty coffee glasses and pushed the two of us out into the yard.

Marcel waved me into the barn. We walked over to the wooden bench where the goose carcasses were lined up, tied up and gleaming clean; he lifted one onto each shoulder then nodded at me to do the same. He led me out of the barn, into the courtyard and up a flight of steps attached to the outside of the cowshed. At the top of the stairs he led me through a large, old, wooden door. I followed him into the middle of the room and watched as he attached his geese to pieces of string hanging from a roof beam. I got the nod again so did the same.

We carried out this procedure until all the geese were suspended across the room in a line. They looked naked and exposed hanging in that dusty, dark place. I started to look around the rooms; it became obvious that this was where Marcel had lived before he built the farmhouse.

There was a kitchen, some bedrooms and a living room, all on the same level. The floors were wooden, the walls roughly plastered. There were no ceilings, just roof beams, and everything was covered in a thick layer of grey dust. Marcel watched me walk from room to room. In one bedroom I saw children's books and toys, in another school books. Marcel wrote a date in the dust, '1979', then looked at me. I turned and looked at this big wooden loft above the cow barn that had been roughly divided into rooms. I knew his two children; they were married and modern, but they had been children here, in this place that looked like a poster for a Dickens' play. I was not going to show Marcel my shock; I knew he would feel shameful when he had no need to. Little did he know, we had a lot in common. His family had lived here until 1979 with no bathroom or electric, and one tap. Nothing had changed here for a century.

Then Marcel had built his farmhouse, with bathrooms and electric, central heating and fridges, double glazing and duvets, sofas and wardrobes; they had stepped from one century to another overnight.

We left this museum, walked back down the wooden steps, across the courtyard and towards the kitchen for coffee. As usual I walked behind him to save me the embarrassment of not being able to talk. I looked back at the place above the cow shed, then forwards at his farmhouse, across his well laid-out fields that made up his farm, and then at his back. He was a small man, no more that five foot; at that moment he looked about ten foot to me.

The coffee glasses were already on the table. I sat down. Marcel went over to a sideboard, took out a bottle of something mauve and poured each of us a large dram. The rest of the afternoon sailed by.

After dinner that night, Viveka wanted to hear more about the geese and the fire.

"After we had hung up the last goose, he called it 'foie gras' and patted its chest. What's foie gras?" I asked her

"You won't find it in pie and mash!"

"Your so continental!" I said and sulked.

Victoria came marching into the kitchen, raised herself to her full two foot eight inches and announced she was not going back to that school as every lunch time they made her wear a bib.

"I'm too big for a bib," she said and looked sad.

I wandered outside to plan a vegetable patch.

Three mornings a week, the bread delivery man drove past our house and down towards the farmhouse blowing his hooter; the kids scrambled out of the door to collect the bread (or was it the bags of sweets ?). Viv and I watched from the kitchen window; Victoria skipped quickly down the lane, Keira crawled after her as fast as she could. Madam, or Mamie as the kids had started to call her, walked up the lane and picked up Keira, took Victoria's hand, then walked back to the bread van. Marcel was leaning on the side of the van chatting to Claude. I said to Viv:

"I bet his moaning about the price of bread!"

Mamie tucked her bread under her arm, looked at Marcel which meant 'you're paying for the bread', then took the children into her kitchen. And that's all we saw of them until lunchtime. The boss, however, stayed gossiping and laughing with the bread man, hoping he'd forget about the payment no doubt.

Victoria was spending more and more time down at the farm; we encouraged her, as we had no real friends or relatives here, and Marcel and Evette were making great adoptive grandparents. Plus the longer she spent with French people, the quicker she would learn the language, we thought. What we didn't know was that, when the girl's were there, Marcel and Evette only spoke Patois to each other.

We had been in France for a few months without a telly or phone; none of us seemed to miss them. If we wanted to make a call, the phone box in the village did the job, as long as you had a bag of coins. It was from this phone box that I kept in touch with the Sloane ranger, but after the last few calls I thought to myself:

'I've got to get rid of her.'

I met Marcel and Trio in Villautou. I was looking at that house Trio had told me to buy, thinking: 'Perhaps I could buy it, do it up, then, just before we leave, sell it and go home with a few bob.'

Trio obviously read my mind. He ripped the 'For Sale' sign off the house, pulled me into the phone box, put his half round glasses on, read the phone number on the torn sign and dialled it. He spoke for two minutes then handed me the receiver. A lady with a strong Germanic accent started telling me, in English, we could buy the house if her first husband agreed the price; I told her as long as I agreed as well, we could talk. She said she would come over the next day and that's what she did. Viveka and I were led around the half-house, half-ruin, then found ourselves standing in the tiny garden alone.

"If you buy it you realise that's all our money gone," Viv said.

I walked her back to the house then turned her around and pointed to the view.

"Buy it! We'll eat cake!" she said.

As Viv's German was better than the German lady's English, the price was negotiated in German. When they had both agreed, Viv, Victoria, Keira and me were driven to the solicitor by the German lady. He had an office in a town ten minutes away and, to my surprise, was waiting for us. His secretary led us into a small waiting room. After a few minutes the German lady became very restless. Eventually we were shown into his office. The German lady sat down with a huff, he looked up and asked her in good English if she was quite well. I thought he looked like an eagle; his office was neat and precise just like him. He started to describe the procedure about buying a house in France; I knew that Viv would listen to his every word so I started dreaming about my new house. When he had finished I asked him how long it would be before we could move in.

"Three months minimum," he said.

I looked at the German woman.

"Viv, ask her if there's any reason why this sale would fall through."

"Nein," madam Frau answered.

"Then if I give this solicitor all the money now, instead of just the deposit, could we move in, start work and sign the final contract when it arrives?"

"Jar," she said.

The solicitor looked shocked but before he could express his professional misgivings, gave him a cheque, signed the contract and escorted all of us back to my new house.

Back at the house, Madam Frau gave me the key, and then she went back to the other side of France. My family and me stood in the huge kitchen surrounded by bricks and rubble, no electric or water, me thinking about where to start. Trio appeared from nowhere and gave us a dead rabbit, so we took it home and watched Marcel skin it.

My daughter was right to complain about the school she was going to; she should have been attending a school much nearer to where we lived, the school that covered our area, the school with kids her own age. And that's where we were now, the wife talking to the headmistress and only teacher rolled into one. The classroom looked like my old one: rows of lift- up desks with inkwells, a blackboard and a globe. One room for all of the kids, all age groups, all being taught by one person, but no ordinary person; this lady in front of us was formidable. I didn't see our girl being much of a problem for her.

"When can she start?" inquired Viv

"Tomorrow."

And that's exactly what happened. The next day Victoria, spick and span and nervous, stood at the bottom of our lane waiting for the school bus to arrive. It arrived on time. Only it wasn't a bus, it was a very large, very old car: shiny and polished, but old. It was packed with children, all crammed in, not a safety belt in sight. The car stopped. From the driver's window a young man turned his head out over his resting elbow and gave us a grin whilst puffing on a giant yellow cigarette. A door swung open; two children leapt out, took our daughter by the hand, led her into the back of the car and sat her in-between them. The car turned and went off up the lane. We watched it travel along the round ridge road, down a dip, then up and out of sight. The wife went in to start the lunch and worry, I went down to the farm; the boss and me had a job on.

A veg patch, the boss was going to make me a veg patch. I had been following him around his one for weeks, he slowly letting me do more work. I reckon he got fed up with me always trailing behind him. One day he walked to the side of my house, pointed to an area of flat ground and said.

"Potagé?"

So I went out and bought chicken wire, made some posts to support it, and now his ancient tractor was throbbing away outside our house.

I liked it when he got the tractor out; he would become even more animated, jumping around and giving orders. Then he would stop with his hands on his hips, directing me on to another job, me twice the size of him attentive and obeying keenly. He was back up on his tractor now, moving to the side of the house: a rotovator attached to the back of the tractor was lowered down onto the flat piece of grassy ground that was to become *my* 'veg patch.' Marcel's hands on the steering wheel, elbows out, head down, accelerator down and he was off!

After a few minutes he started looking back at that rotovator and shaking his head. Then the look on his face changed; I had seen that look before so knew something was up. He stopped, got down off the tractor, put his hands on his hips and cursed Trio. The wife felt the change of tempo and came out of the kitchen drying her hands. I whispered out of the side of my mouth:

"What's the matter with him?"

Translating his ravings, the wife told me: Trio had sold him this hopeless piece of machinery a couple of weeks before, and he was about to drag it back over to his farm and rotovate the top of Trio's head with it! I just wanted a veg patch. Marcel saw my disappointed look, got back up on the tractor and tried again. He stopped again, looked back at me then indicated I was to stand on the top of the rotovator while he drove. I jumped up, he set off. Must have been getting the right result because the green grass was turning into brown earth behind us.

We carried on for another half an hour, then the tractor stopped in front of Mamie. It was her turn to have her hands on her hips. I didn't need the wife to translate; she wanted to know why Marcel was cutting the earth up and downwards and not across-ways? The rain will wash every thing away rotovating like this, she said, was he a complete moron (polite translation.)? I reckoned the boss had just become confused in his rage about Trio, and if Trio was in trouble before, his life was in danger now.

After a couple of hours the job was done; I had a patch of brown, sideways ploughed ground behind my house. I heard the school bus pull up. We all ran over to the road; Viv, Mamie, Marcel and me. Victoria jumped out, socks rolled down, jacket slung over her shoulder, and jumped into our arms. Marcel and Mamie went down to the farm for lunch, we went indoors to ours.

My daughter chatted excitedly; she had made a friend, had her own desk and played in the playground; the driver had sung to the children all the way to school and back. Keira still didn't have a high chair so we passed food to her under the table.

After lunch, back to the veg patch to dig a trench ten inches deep all around the edge for the bottom of the fence, so that the rabbits couldn't get under. Got all the posts into the ground, then started to get the chicken wire up: this was awkward and tiring. Eventually had the wire in place, the gate working and the earth around the bottom of the fence pushed back into place.

Leant on my shovel and looked up. I could see the sky from one horizon to the other; a bright, scarlet coloured, cloudless sky silhouetting the Pyrenees, the stars already appearing on the other horizon and, hanging in front of me, the moon, almost too bright to look at. I could smell the earth on my hands and the first drops of dew in my hair.

Marcel appeared and had a good look at my work; I knew it wasn't up to his standards, but he nodded, grinned, clapped me on the back, and then went into his own vegetable patch. Struck the shovel into the ground, walked to the door of the house and called for everybody to come out. They wandered out curiously, wondering what I wanted. I took them to the side of the house and showed them the moon and sky, opened my new gate, took everybody inside, and explained where I intended to plant peppers and aubergines, strawberries and carrots, lettuce and beetroot, beans and tomatoes, and rows and rows of potatoes, my excitement growing with visions of fresh home grown food for us to eat.

Viv had disappeared after a few minutes, so me and the kids sat and looked at the moon. After a while, Viv called us up for dinner; she had pulled the dining table outside and covered it with one of her new recipes. I sat down and ate with an appetite I didn't know existed. After this feast, the kids staggered indoors to bed; Viv and I sat outside in the hot air, under the bright moon and finished the wine.

With the money I had left after paying for the new house and the little bit of rent money I received from London, I reckoned I could employ the poet for two months. Enough to get me started, then I would have to think of another way to feed Viv and the kids. I phoned him and arranged to meet at the house on the following Monday morning.

'Great,' I thought, 'a week to arrange my vegetable patch.'

A few days before phoning the hippie, I had taken the children to the local riding club to watch a small show jumping contest. We sat close by the rails near one of the bigger fences. There was a rider going round getting ready, warming up, getting the horse's attention; a bell rang and she was off!

After watching them complete several jumps, I felt myself being pulled towards them; I stopped hearing the crowd, all I could see was the horse. My heart started to beat furiously as I became captivated by the sight before me. The horse came thundering up to the jump nearest to me, the rider wide eyed and concentrating, the horse sweating, the rider trying desperately to communicate by using her reigns and legs; a heart stopping moment as the horse approached the fence, the thud as his front hooves hit the floor, the lurch as the great beast prepared to take off, then, in that perfect split second, the rider committing himself to the fence, the breathtaking sight of horse and rider going up and through the air and over the fence. They both landed in a flash of colour and pounded earth, then on to next fence. I was thunderstruck! I wanted to be that rider, I wanted to jump fences with a massive, sweat-covered horse.

I sat there for the whole event, not once taking my eyes off the horses, the longing to be up there with them becoming an ache.

At the end of the competition, I wandered around amongst the horseboxes, watching the cavaliers packing up their equipment and feeding, grooming and wrapping up their horses. I stroked their manes and fell hopelessly in love.

I was alongside a particularly spectacular horse when one of the riders came up beside me and said:

"She's beautiful isn't she?"

I nodded, transfixed.

"Why don't you come here and ride?" she said.

"Yes," I said, "why don't I?"

The next day I went back to find out the cost. It was so cheap I joined and paid for ten lessons, a decision that would change my life forever, a decision that brought me so much happiness, and pain; a decision that at times would help to keep me sane.

"I've joined the riding club," I told Viv

"Yes dear, I thought you might."

That afternoon, Marcel came up to our house and asked if I could give him a hand. We went back down to the farm then up to his barn, took the geese down from the hooks, then out to the farm yard to put them onto the back of the tractor's trailer.

Clean white paper was spread out over the wooden planks. The geese lay on the paper, the boss taking great care over laying them out. He fussed and fretted, moved them an inch, tucked their heads up, then let them hang down, rubbed the yellow skin on their backs, pinched out the last of any tiny feathers that he imagined were there. If I touched or moved anything he would move it back. He was becoming more and more nervous. I didn't know why.

Job done, we sat on the back of the trailer. He didn't say anything, I just thought he was waiting for something.

A long black Mercedes slid onto the road at the far end of the farm. Marcel just turned one ear in its direction; I knew he wouldn't be able to see it, but he could hear something coming onto that road long before I could. Just before the car drove into the farmyard, he stood up with his hands on his hips. Mamie had not appeared; I thought that odd.

The car came to a stop in front of the tractor. A city slicker beamed out of the car; the boss shook his hand, then turned to the geese. I leant against the barn wall.

Their conversation started friendly enough, the city slicker squeezing the geese one after the other, too hard I thought. After each squeeze, a comment; then the boss would shake his head. Another squeeze, another comment, another shaking of the head. Marcel was starting to turn red. I realised this white-suited, flat-shoed scorpion had come to buy the geese, and whatever he was saying made the boss very angry; Marcel might be small, with a face lined and browned with age, but angry he would frighten most people. I thought about the shotgun hanging in the scullery. I had a vision of the city slicker disappearing with his Merc into a large hole in the Pyrenees.

Their talk had turned into an eyeball-to-eyeball screaming match. The boss looked about to explode, his neck had swollen to twice its normal size, and the slicker was screaming into the boss' face. I pushed myself off the wall and started to walk between them; they both turned and looked at me, looked at each other, looked at the geese. The tension subsided as quickly as it erupted, the city boy dug his hand into his pocket and pulled out a huge wad of Franc notes, the temperature rose briefly during the counting. Then a long flick-knife appeared in the slicker's hands. My stomach tightened. He grabbed one of the birds and slit it open, pulled the two halves apart, and they both looked in; the boss slapped the slicker on the back, the slicker laughed and slapped the boss on the back, I laughed and was told to put the geese into the slicker's car.

After all the fun, Mamie appeared and told me to go up to my house, get Viv and the girls, and come down to the farm. So that's what I did. We were all sat round the kitchen table with the little glasses in front of us waiting to be filled with coffee, the slicker at the opposite end of the table to the boss and me next to the boss; I was happy about that. During coffee, the boss produced a bottle of rum and a tot was put in the men's glasses, extra biscuits for the ladies and baby. The talk was elevated and fun. Marcel was about to give the boys another dram, he got a look from Mamie, so sat back down again.

The coffee break over, we all walked the slicker back to his car. He opened the boot, counted and checked the geese, then opened the driver's door, flopped into his seat and skidded off in a cloud of grit. Marcel walked into his vet patch to count his money. Mamie came with us; she wanted to have a gossip with Viv and get out of her kitchen for a bit. As we walked she told us it was the same ritual every year; the slicker was from Marseille and he came to buy the geese livers. The boss would never let him cut the geese open and see what he wanted to buy until they had agreed a price and the slicker had paid. Every year they nearly came to blows about the hidden liver's size and quality; after cutting open the goose, the slicker always agreed the boss produced the best fois gras in the area.

Viv and Mamie walked into the kitchen, I walked back and looked through the fence around Marcel's vegetable patch. He was hidden, immersed in his tomatoes, but I could hear his chuckle.

Over the next few months, I started work on the house with the hippie. There was no bathroom or toilet, no kitchen and the place was full of rubble; the German lady and her husband had obviously started to convert the house then just walked out. I planned four bedrooms, a kitchen, dining room, office, living room and small garden. The hippie told me that before any of that we needed a new roof.

"Yes," he said making a roll up, "we will have this place finished in a year."

'At your pace, a year; at mine, three months!' I thought.

The new roof was on in three days, the hippie seemed to be angry.

"That normally takes three weeks," he grunted.

'Yeah, especially when you're being paid by the hour,' I thought.

He realised at this rate the place would be finished faster then he would like; tea breaks became more frequent, he tried to keep conversations going but as we had nothing in common, he just sulked. I grinned and thought:

'A few more weeks and I'll have learnt enough about building not to need him.' Besides, money was running away and the recession at home seemed to be getting worse.

I had given everybody I knew in England the number of the village phone box and told them they could only phone me in the daytime when I was working. I was slowly giving the hippie less and less work and doing more myself. We were in mid-winter. There were holes in most of the walls for the plumbing; the cold breeze seeped through them, up my legs and seemed to get stuck in my hands.

I had been mixing cement by hand as the hippie had taken his mixer home; I was frozen, just wanted to get this last load mixed and onto the wall, it was getting dark so had to hurry. The phone in the call box started to ring. Wiped my hands, walked across the street into the box, lifted the phone and a voice said:

"Mr Griffiths?"

"You dialled the number," I said wearily.

It was one of my tenants; although they were decent people, they had proved to be completely undomesticated, unable to do the simplest chore.

"The light in the bathroom doesn't work,"

"Have you switched it on?" I said sarcastically and thought of the warm centrally heated house he was phoning from

"Yes," he said innocently

"Then the bulb's gone, you will have to change it," I said, freezing cement dripping of the ends of my fingers

"I can't do that; you must, you're the landlord!"

"I'm a thousand miles away, in the middle of nowhere and you want me to change your light bulb?" I said slumping against the glass wall of the phone box

"We have to be able to use the bathroom!"

"Go and wait in the living room," I said and put the receiver down.

I phoned a friend with the last of the change I had.

"John, go round to my house and change a light bulb for me."

"You are joking of course?"

"No, go and do it then phone me back, I've got no change left."

Put the receiver down and dripped back to work.

Got the last of the cement on the wall, cleaned up, ate some sweets, went outside and stood in the phone box.

'I can't believe those people,' I thought, 'can't change a light bulb!' The phone rang, I picked up the receiver.

"That dozy bastard you've got round there couldn't blow his own nose," said my angry friend, "He said he's going to take the cost of the phone call he made to you off the rent. And I noticed your house is in a right state."

He was working up a head of steam now, I didn't want him going back round there, 'to have a word' as he would say, so I said:

"How's Chelsea getting on?"

The steam disappeared.

"Beat Arsenal yesterday," he beamed.

We talked for half an hour; I was transported home in my head, standing in a warm pub, chatting to a mate about football over a pint of Guiness. It was pitch black and freezing cold outside so kept John talking as long as I could.

"This is costing me a bleeding fortune! See you down the pub in half an hour!" he said putting down the phone and laughing his head off.

COCKNEY IN CORBIERE | 109

I slowly put the receiver down and turned round; Trio had his face pressed up against the glass door. I felt homesick.

We had been visited several times by one of the local policeman, the hippie had introduced us in a bar. The policeman asked where I lived and then started calling round socially. He was fat, young and obviously thought himself a bit of a Romeo. The visits had become more and more frequent. One day at work I mentioned it to the hippie.

"He's checking you out to see if you're up to no good or running away," he said

"You mean he visits all the new comers?"

"He supposed to be big in drugs," the hippies eyes looking at me with suspicion.

'It's the accent again,' I thought, 'as soon as they hear the cockney accent they think you're a great train robber!'

"Good job he never looked in the room under the garage then," I said, and walked back to work.

'All that cosser's interested in,' I thought, 'is the wife; the hippie needs a trip back to blighty!'

A few days after this enlightening chat with the hippie, I had gone into town to buy some wood. It was market day, so parked the car and trailer, and then walked into one of the small cafés near the centre square. The copper was sat at one of the tables, filling his belly with croissants. I sat next to him and let him talk. Behind and to his right through the glass window I could see a bunch of brown ricers smoking huge joints and selling their crop to the locals. I turned and asked the drugs buster if there was a local drug problem.

"Not in this town, never seen anything like that."

Through the glass, the scruffiest one with a massive beard was about to leave. He passed a small packet to someone at the next table and floated out with his mates.

Mr Plod was eyeing my croissant, so I got up from the table, put my coat on, said goodbye and turned round to leave, stopped, turned back, picked up the croissant, grinned at the flic and ate it.

Driving back I stopped at the riding stables to pat the horse I had started to ride.

The riding stable was tiny: about ten boxes, a manège and a tiny corral. The riding instructor was beautiful. The bread man's daughter had taken the place over from the previous tenants and was employing the young lady to give riding instructions.

The day I walked in to sign up, they had only been open for a week. I was one of their first pupils. It meant that for months I got one-to-one training, so made good enough progress to start jumping and plan my first competition. After the first few weeks my eldest daughter wanted to start riding too; I hoped we would ride together one day. The instructress was from a large town an hour away. Because of her good looks she was receiving a lot of attention from the local people. She only seemed to be interested in horses and teaching.

From my first lesson, her enthusiasm was obvious; this was her first job and she was going to give it her best shot. After a few months, more and more people were coming for lessons, but as I started early to have the day clear for work, Viv and the kids, I still got personal attention and fell more in love with horses. I hadn't seen much of the hippie for a while, the copper had disappeared.

During spring we had run into, been introduced to, or opened the door to several English people; as the area was so remote we were surprised how many there were. The first one to turn up was a lady living with her three sons in a big house ten minutes away. Her car pulled up in front of our house; we were sitting on our small veranda at teatime when this white, battered Fiat clunked into view. From the car, a very butch looking lady in huge furry boots emerged and came striding towards us, thrusting her hand at Viveka who I knew wouldn't take it, so I stood up quickly and shook the end of it. She sat down and talked in a loud, high-pitched voice, endlessly, until Marcel appeared around the front of the house, walked across the garden and into my vegetable patch.

"Who's he?" she squeaked

"The boss, the landlord's father." I answered,

"Is this the sort of thing you have to put up with? Invasion of privacy if you ask me! He can't walk around your place like this. You pay rent. Shouldn't be allowed," she said in that high-pitched, irritated voice.

Then she glared towards the vegetable patch looking angry.

I thought: 'Viveka is not going to like this woman!'

Took furry boots over to meet the boss. The old sod flashed his blue eyes at her and flirted. Furry boots got back into her car and drove off. I walked back to the veranda to finish my tea. Viv had cleared everything away, and I knew that meant furry boots as well.

Through the hippie we met an artist and invited him round for dinner one evening. He arrived with his young lady, nineteen years his junior. They were a happy couple. She still lived in London, going to university; he lived in a village forty minutes away from us.

During the dinner we learnt why he was here.

"For seventeen years I taught art at a leading university; some of my pupils went on to become successful painters. I painted part-time but always had the ambition to be a full time artist. After a long and wonderful trip to France with my wife, I realised I wanted to live there and try to become a professional artist. I told her my dream and asked her if she'd join me. She said: 'go and we divorce."

He delivered this little speech pissed.

I looked at the young, pretty girl at his side and thought she was ample comfort for him whilst the divorce went through. During the evening we discovered we had a mutual love of sport, art, music, books and beauty. We became instant friends and still are.

I was really enjoying the building work on the house; after sitting inside the London dungeon repairing jewellery for years it was great to use my body. I was on my own too. When I started building, I couldn't even mix cement; I had learnt to pick up heavy weights with the minimum of effort, to keep my tools clean and always try working out how to go about the next days work the night before. I had to force myself to work at a slower pace; I had to think about what I was doing rather than hurtle around on autopilot, and when I took a break I could lie in the sun and adore the mountains.

Days went by without me seeing anyone except Viv, my girls and their new adopted grandma and grandpa. I worked in the vegetable patch at night and rode my beautiful horse three mornings a week. At the weekends I took the family to the sea or on long walks through the Pyrenees. We still had no phone or telly and as nobody seemed to miss them I didn't mention it. I was quietly becoming very happy.

As money became tighter and tighter, I learned not to waste a thing: straightening nails to reuse them, keeping stones, rubble and earth, which could all be used for something. Wherever I was, if I saw a discarded piece of wood or useful-looking piece of metal, I stopped and collected it, thinking one day it might save me money.

The physical work, as well as the horse riding, started to change the shape of my body. I started to walk to work from the farm to the village. The distance between the two was about five kilometres along a road which led me through fields full of sunflowers, past meadows crammed with wild flowers and cows, passed bird-filled hedgerows twittering with colour, the misty, dew-filled air making me feel heady and healthy.

The house started to look like the inside of an English country cottage; Viveka designed the important parts, the cottage bit was her doing. I cleared the garden and planned the layout, pencilling in the vegetable patch first, then trees and scrubs. I wanted most things to bear some sort of fruit; growing something just to look at seemed to be a waste.

Marcel's dog had adopted us too; he followed the kids everywhere, or they followed him I was never sure. He was huge, kind and parental with them, and he made them and us feel safe. During the week, when the kids went to school, he started to join me on my walk to work. He ran in front of me, his great tail upright and swishing with glee. He stuck his head in the bushes and plodded after bees and butterflies, all the while grinning and looking for rabbits or cats. Wild cats in the area had become a problem; to the dog they were fair game. He always stopped when we got to the field of cows, sat down and stared at them. I used to stand behind him and wonder what he was thinking.

Our walk took us down a steep hill where the Marie's secretary's house nestled at the bottom. The road passed close to her front door. On the other side of the road, a row of high, closely packed conifers stood in a long line. She had a big, white cat that used to hide behind the conifers. The dog walked in front of me along the tarmac road and when we got to the conifers he would listen out for the cat. As the trees were thick and close together, even if he heard the cat he could never push himself through quickly enough; the cat always escaped.

One morning, as we descended the hill towards the secretary's house, I was sure my doggie friend was grinning. As we approached the first tree he shot around the outside. There was a frenzied, scurrying sound so I shouted his name; the response was a loud crunching noise followed by silence. He emerged at the far end of the trees, prancing with his tail in the air, beaming from ear to ear. I ran off quickly; he looped in front of me, turning his huge head to smile at me. The next day I found the remains of the cat and hid them. The secretary asked me twice if I had seen the cat; both times she asked me, she made a point of looking at the dog. If I didn't love him so much I would have shopped him. I was so embarrassed.

Money was running out but the vegetable patch was blooming; I had planted peppers, aubergines and chillies which the boss said would not grow.

"The summer isn't long enough; they're for the med!"

I ignored him and planted them along with the tomatoes, strawberries, French beans, lettuce, beetroot, onions, garlic and, right in the middle of all this, a peach tree.

The boss showed me how to rotovate the land for potatoes.

After I had worked the soil for days, he took me off to the market to buy seed potatoes. After inspecting every potato in the market, he selected the trader selling the cheapest ones, then started to haggle. I eventually bought two sacks full.

"Put those in the garage until next Saturday," he said

"Why don't we plant them today?" I said

"Because there's no full moon," he said

"Yeah of course, Marcel," I said, "must have a full moon."

Visions of blood-sucking potatoes passed in front of me.

'I'll need Viveka to translate here,' I thought so went into the house with Marcel and said:

"Ask him, what are we doing?"

The boss sat down with Viveka and explained: if you planted one row of potatoes every night, starting with the first night of the full moon, the rows would grow as if you had planted them at four week intervals. Then the potatoes wouldn't all be ready at once; you could go and dig up fresh ready potatoes every day to eat, as long as the moon is not allowed to shine on the potatoes or they will stay green. You must be careful to keep them covered until they're under the ground. He said all this with a straight face; I thought he and Trio would be hiding and laughing their heads off watching me planting by moonlight. Even so, I did what I was told: went out for the next five nights and planted the potatoes keeping the moons rays off them, straining my ears for the slightest titter.

'If they're watching me and laughing I'll let his hunting dogs out,' I thought. But after the fifth night not a sound; it was going to take months before I knew if the boss was taking the mick.

The rest of the fruit and vegetables had all done very well; my veg patch was full of ripe Mediterranean fare. The kids helped me every night to water and weed, they ate their way around all the different treats, Keira's face often disappearing inside the bigger tomato's. I had rows of tomatoes all ripening at once so I started to pot them and make tomato ketchup, green tomato chutney and dry the remainder in the sun.

## CHAPTER FOUR

We had been in France for a year and were enjoying every moment of it. Viveka never mentioned going back, so I didn't. We had very little money and hardly any income from the rents in London, so visits to the supermarket were becoming less and less frequent. Viveka never bought pre-packed, frozen, tinned, or dehydrated foods anymore as it was too expensive; she prepared all of our meals using every scrap from the vegetable patch. We ate only the occasional piece of meat or fish. We changed our habits with money; all material things came second to buying essentials for the vegetable patch, petrol for the car or building materials for the house. I rode whenever I could afford it, and worked on the house in the day and the vegetable patch at night.

Victoria spoke good French and still skipped off to school. We had arranged a birthday party for her so that she could invite her new school friends and some local kids. The invitations were posted and the replies came back swiftly, all of them accepting. Viv and I spent days making preparations; Viv baked cakes, cast jellies and made paper decorations, including a new birthday tablecloth. We guessed agricultural kids couldn't be kept indoors, whatever the weather, so my job was making the games for the children to play outside. I made bobbing apples and sitting ducks on a small artificial pond; I hid the treasure and drew the maps for the hunt, put fresh sand in the pit and Marcel cut the grass around the house (his idea: "snakes won't crawl through short grass," he lectured).

The children arrived in the back of their parents' car, all dressed up in their Sunday best. The back door opened, the spotless child jumped out and the car sped off with a parental hand waving from the driver's window. The children gathered in quiet groups on Marcel's front lawn. When the last child arrived and the last parental hand had waved goodbye, I took all of the children over to the bobbing apples, pleading with them not to get too wet.

We all played 'til Viveka called everybody in to eat. The children ran past my semi-submerged head, laughing and screaming with hunger. Viveka had laid a table with her homemade cakes, jam and jelly. There were streamers, hats, coloured paper hanging from the ceiling and bunting strung from corner to corner. I walked into the living room, wiping my head with a towel, quickly glanced around and realised how birthday decorations were a new thing for these children. I went across to the birthday spread, looked at the children and waved my arms at the chairs. The children rushed towards me and jostled for a seat near the big cake. Viv picked up the huge knife laid by the side of the cake and smoothly sliced it into the right amount of segments; the room became very silent as each child waited for their slice of this delicious cake to plop onto their plate. After the last slice was plopped, Viv picked up a huge bowl of whipped cream topped with strawberries and each slice of cake was ladled with a helping. The children's patience was admirable, but their bulging eyes and salivating lips told a different story. After their glasses were filled with lemonade, me and Viv left them to it and went into the kitchen for a cup of tea. After a couple of minutes Viv said:

"It's very quiet in there."

"Good!" I said holding my cup out to be filled with more tea

"It's not good," Viv said and led me back into the living room.

None of the children had touched their food.

'They don't like Viv's cake!' I thought and panicked.

All the kids were sat still, not saying a word.

I called Victoria over and asked her what the problem was.

"They won't start to eat until you say so, dad!"

So I sort of rolled my arms around each other and nodded my head. There was a gentle stirring of forks and spoons, then the children started, very delicately, to eat their food. I had never seen a group of such well-behaved children! Viv and I stood and watched them eat, feeling relieved there was nothing wrong.

"Can I have that other cup of tea now?" I said grinning at Viv

"No," she said, "go outside and get the rest of the games ready. The children will soon eat this lot!"

I went outside to put the tail on the donkey and the ducks on the small artificial pond.

When the kids had finished eating they rushed out and waited for me to organise them and explain to them how to play the games; to most of these kids, organised games were a new experience. It was only after a few minutes I sensed there was something different about the way these kids played games. After I had herded the children round to the fourth or fifth game, I knew what the difference was between the children I'd known in central London and this lot. It was the way they helped each other capture the duck, retrieve the apple, pin the tail in the right place. Nobody was winning and nobody was losing. There were no hysterics, only soft laughter at some child's lack of ability, followed by gentle encouragement. I left them to the treasure hunt in the secure knowledge that the smaller children would be protected by the larger ones. I walked into the house, past the kitchen and noticed Viv had her arms buried in a mountain of foaming white bubbles. The living room had been cleared so I pushed the table out into the hallway, collected all the chairs and put them down the centre of the room. I dragged out my old record player, plugged it in, put a Chas and Dave record on, went back outside and waited.

Over the next half an hour, I occasionally saw children running over fields or behind barns, hooting with laughter and chasing around looking for hidden treasure. They eventually all appeared back on Marcel's lawn to examine the coloured trinkets they had uncovered on the treasure hunt. I waited for the excitement to die down and then told Victoria and Keira to bring all the children into the living room.

"There's nothing for us to do in there!" Victoria said

"Musical chairs!" I said, "we're going to play musical chairs."

The children were sat in the living room, staring at the line of alternating chairs. I explained the rules to Victoria in English, she then explained the rules to the children in French. Once the children were stood in a large circle around the line of chairs, I went across to the record player thinking,

'Let's see how they cope with this!'

I turned the music on and Victoria led the children in a laughing dance around the chairs. After a minute or so, I lifted the needle off the record and the children sat down as they had been told to do. But of course, as the rules dictate, this left one of them standing. Two of the children immediately stood up and offered this child their chair. These children had never played an organised competitive game in their lives and simply didn't understand the meaning of it! They only understood competing with the elements, keeping back and fighting against nature; games were for city people with energy to spare. I felt like the foreign settler bringing in tuberculosis. These kids made my life's obsession with competitive games look ridiculous. Their gentleness was bred into them by generations of people farming impossible land, whose competitive instincts were sated by their work. They fought against nature, not each other. Nature was a far bigger opponent than bobbing apples or floating ducks. These children belittled, this was the strangest game of musical chairs I had ever witnessed. Nobody lost or won. The children just kept on dancing around the chairs no matter how many there were. When the music stopped they would dive at the remaining chairs; the ones left standing just waited for the music to start again. We had tried to tell the chairless ones they were out of the game, but the remaining children thought that a stupid idea and went and brought the children back to play. When there were no chairs left they just danced. I gave up and took them outside to play the last game, 'It', consisting of everyone being 'it'. This allowed the children to run, jostle and poke the frustration of musical chairs away.

By the time the parents arrived to pick their children up, the children were dusty, dirty, stuffed and happy. For them, the long afternoon at the foreigners' house was over. They were happy and slightly confused. I think after the party we became even more alien to them; they found us exotic but strange. My heart felt jittery at the thought of these remote children joining the outside world, as one day they must. The land here wouldn't support them. I wanted to protect them, although I knew I couldn't. I might be strange here, but I had lived all my life in a place they would have to go to, a place so far away from the way of life here I feared the worst. I wanted to give them all I knew, empty my head into theirs, show them how to keep the wolves away, prepare them for when they leave this forgotten haven. Perhaps we did in our small way, but it was years before I saw the influence we had on their lives. Some stayed, some left to live in the big cities. The letters we get from the ones in the outside world are full of hope and happiness; the ones that stayed have a problem, it's still waiting there, a journey into modern life. Avoiding it can only cause self-doubt. But right now it was their turn to teach me, show me a life I didn't understand, help me see that the ways of the city boy can look stupid and silly, unfulfilling; the real rewards were in seeing the things nature laid out in front of me. The day became a humbling experience that elevated my spirits and then at the end of the day a deep happiness and the kindling of understanding filled me.

Victoria and Keira were very excited, it took ages to get them to settle down. I told them endless stories, then they'd ask for just one more.

Eventually they were finally asleep.

Viv and I had another cup of tea. We sat amongst the bunting and talked about the day, about the games and musical chairs, the happiness and laughter the kids had brought into our house and how our girls had enjoyed the whole day.

"One more cup of tea then bed for me, luv," I said yawing

"The children were lovely, weren't they?" Viv said and stared at me

"Yes a great day," I said and stared back

"Kids *are* lovely, yes, they are lovely kids," she said repeating herself then grinned at me

"They are," I nodded and thought she had said 'lovely' and 'kids' once too often

"Lovely," she said and grinned and stared again, "it's lovely with loads of kids."

I put my tea cup on the table, smiled at her and said:

"When is it due?"

She looked down and whispered:

"In seven months. I'm sorry, I know we're broke."

I raced around to her side of the table, knelt down and put my hand on her belly.

"You don't mind?" she whispered while stroking my hair

Since our relationship started we had never used contraception. There was an unspoken acceptance that if Viv became pregnant, that would be fine. But for years there had been no sign of a baby. Eventually we went to see a specialist who said:

"Something is wrong!"

He would have to give us both tests.

We thought about that for a couple of days then decided it was too much of a risk; if he found something wrong with one of us that he could not cure, we would know the truth, and who was to blame. We thought we would let God decide.

Now we were about to have our third baby.

I loved it when Viv was pregnant; with the first baby I was so ambitious I used to rub oil into her belly every night. I was so proud of her and her roundness. I used to catch her standing side-ways in front of mirrors. I bought her maternity dresses, all flowers and bows, and took her everywhere. I wanted people to see how lovely she was; I thought she was the most perfect thing I had ever seen, and the sexiest.

And now I was to have it all again.

"Do you want a boy?" Viv said and looked anguished

"Three girls will do just fine." I said, picking her up and taking her to bed.

One night, after dragging myself home from work covered in dust and cement, I staggered through the front door and stopped in the hallway to take off my crusty clothes. Viv stood with her back to me, washing up in the kitchen. She turned around from the kitchen sink and said:

"Your roll-ups and poetry book are by the fire."

I changed and went out to the vegetable patch with my two girls. I had never felt better or fitter. After I'd been weeding for a while, Marcel appeared with two tiny shotguns under his arms.

"There's too many rabbits," he said, "come on, we're going hunting!"

The girls went home and I followed him down to the farm. We were to creep across the front of his farmhouse, then sneak up to some bales of hay in which he had made holes to poke the guns through. He had purposely positioned the hay so that it faced the biggest field. From the edge of the farm building we could see the rabbits nibbling at the grass all over his field. He didn't mind them eating the grass, it was the vegetable patch: they still managed to get inside. After having gone to the market, bought the seeds and prepared the ground over several weeks, it drove us mad that, just as the new shots appeared, the rabbits ate them all. He knew just how important the vegetables were to me.

The boss was in front, me behind, both of us bent over in a ridiculously low, crouched position with guns at the ready; we didn't want those rabbits to see us over the top of the bales. We got to the hay and saw the rabbits, poked our guns through the holes and they immediately disappeared. Marcel signalled us to retreat back behind the farmhouse. We crouched back to the edge of the wall and looked up to see that the field was full of rabbits again.

We repeated this manoeuvre at least five times. The sixth time a few rabbits had decided to take their chances and stay out. We raised our guns, took sight and fired; my shot hit a tree between the field and us, his made the water jump in the cows' watering trough. There was a hoot of laughter and clapping from my place. We turned round and looked up; Viv, the kids and Mamie were all looking out of our kitchen window, clapping and laughing at our hopeless efforts. As it was starting to get dark, we thought this was a good time to stop. We signalled to our audience to come down and join us for drinks. We put the guns away, went back out to the courtyard to watch the kids play 'miss the rabbit', and then we all went into Mamie's kitchen for drinks.

Hunting was a proud tradition in these parts so Mamie had great fun telling us that Marcel was a terrible shot. Me and the boss did our pantomime bit, acting out our forlorn hunting skills. Everybody laughed and joined in the miming.

Things quietened down, the kids went out to play, Mamie poured us more coffee. There was a moment's silence. Viv sipped her coffee, put her cup back down on the table, drew in her breath and straightened her back; I knew she was about to say something important.

"Marcel, Evette, there's something I want to tell you: I'm going to have another baby."

I knew why she was nervous: her mother had hardly been thrilled at our latest news. She needed Marcel and Evette's approval and support; they had become very dear to us.

Evette grinned, clapped her hands together, stood up, ran over to Viv and kissed her on both cheeks.

"A baby for the farm!" she said, putting the palms of her hands together and looking upwards, "The best news this year!"

Marcel went to his posh cabinet and took out his finest brandy, poured us both a large dram, offered Mamie one and to our great surprise she took a small nip. Viv had a small glass of red wine. He raised his glass above his head, we all raised our glasses and looked at Marcel.

"To our new French baby!" he said.

We downed our drinks, then he poured him and me another one quickly.

The nights were drawing in; there wasn't much work to do in the vegetable patch. Marcel had been right though; the potatoes had come up at about four week intervals, giving us spuds all summer and most of the winter. My two girls still followed me around, pulling up carrots, digging out potatoes and finishing off the last of the strawberries. One night, one of them called me over and pointed at the beetroots. I looked down, then looked up and called over to Marcel who was weeding in his vegetable patch.

"Come over here and have a look."

He climbed over his fence, then over mine, looked down and chuckled; there, nestled among the beetroot leaves, were four baby rabbits. While we had been out hunting them, they had been giving birth in my vegetable patch! We picked them up and felt their soft downy fur. One of them squeaked like a baby, Marcel looked at me and shook his head. The girls looked at me, pleading with their big blue eyes for mercy. I put the babies back under the beetroot. Marcel went back to weeding. I gathered together the veg we had picked that night, and we left, closing the gate quietly behind us.

Took the veg in to Viv, then me and the girls went up to perfume park to watch the sun go down. I never realised how beautiful, blond, bubbly and bright my daughters were. I never had much time to be with them in London, I hadn't realised children could be such good company. I felt happy and lucky. As I sat watching them, I realised how quickly they had adapted to country life. I thought school and the language would have been a big problem, but both of them had taken it all in their stride. Victoria went off in the school bus everyday, Keira had started nursery. They both went without a backwards glance. At the weekends and during school holidays, they ran around the fields without a care. Viv looked after us all and blossomed.

Then came an unexpected blow.

Black Monday exploded on us, taking interest rates through the roof. The rents wouldn't cover the mortgage. I would have to find money from somewhere to top up the repayments if I wanted to keep the house in London, and to feed the family. That was not going to be easy living in the middle of nowhere, in a foreign country where winter was just around the corner, with no work permit and unable to speak the language properly.

After a couple of days I realised how grave the situation was; there was only enough money in the bank to pay next month's hugely increased mortgage repayment and the rent here, then I would be left completely skint.

'That fucking fat chancellor needs skinning alive,' I thought, 'bet he wouldn't go without one big fat dinner, the fat bastard!'

Tens of thousands of people were about to lose their houses. Reading the papers from England I knew that the useless, incompetent politicians were still swanning around with their heads in the clouds, not realising the agony they were about to cause. The worst thing was, there was not one word of sympathy from the privileged idiots.

Marcel and two of his local farming friends came down to the house in the village to look at my work. They had arranged to meet Trio in the village and were early. After ten minutes their incredulous looks and shaking heads signalled their incomprehension; they couldn't understand why anybody would want the inside of the house to look five hundred years old. They had spent money they never had, and time they couldn't afford, rebuilding the insides of their old cottages to look modern: plaster board walls, brown tiles, multi-coloured bathroom fittings and, of course, the obligatory solitary light bulb hanging from the middle of each ceiling and six-thousand-inch colour TV in every room. They just thought I didn't know how to do it properly, so once again I had to listen and be told, with a finger wagging in front of my face, how to build a clinic. I reminded them about meeting Trio by the phone box, shuffled them outside and, just to make sure there were no hard feelings, quickly made everybody a cup of coffee, put the cups on a tray and took it out to them.

Trio appeared with his smiling moustache and made eyes at the coffee. We sipped it all the slower just to tease him. To get his own back he said:

"What's all this on the telly about Britain?"

I explained in my pidgin French that the chancellor had doubled interest rates almost over night. They wanted to know everything, so I explained about people being thrown out of their houses.

"Thousands of people will lose their houses because of interest rates?" said Marcel, "What are they going to do about it? You can't put people on the street through no fault of their own."

"It's already happening," I said.

Trio spat on the ground, then said:

"Bankers and politicians; fat-bellied, thieving, useless pigs' arses!"

Everybody nodded. I knew most farmers were in debt to the bank in this poor farming area. They had all made it clear to me what they thought about bankers, or for that matter city people in general. During the farmers' strike a few months earlier, Marcel had said:

"City people: let them cut their stomachs open and eat what comes out if they're hungry!"

We stood in a circle sipping our coffee. Marcel said:

"If England was Pakistan, the media would be asking us for relief money."

As I was responsible for this gloomy mood, I was madly trying to think of something to cheer us up. It appeared: a small, shiny, new French car. It came slowly up the hill into the village the wrong way, the driver ignoring the one-way sign. We knew that meant the driver thought himself above any sign tiny Villautou displayed.

The car pulled up beside us, Marcel and his mates walked over to the phone box pretending to be busy, leaving me on my own to deal with the stranger. A tall, thick set, middle aged, pale-looking, suited man struggled out of the driver's door.

He asked me if I knew were Patrick Viola lived. When I started to answer he heard the accent and looked across at the gathering outside the phone box. My friends turned their backs on him, so he turned to me and repeated his question.

"Where does Mr Viola live?"

He pulled out his clip board and put his pen on it; that really impressed me.

Patrick was the village builder. A big, friendly man. He worked with his brother driving off every day in their old lorry to earn whatever they could in these difficult times. They'd never missed a day's work nor had a holiday in the year I had lived here. Most mornings their flat-backed lorry rattled into the village to pick up some materials or machinery from their yard. I would quickly make coffee then take it out to them, the three of us, three builders, three comedians. It was one of the day's highlights. Patrick's wife rode horses. She, a shy lady, rode across our Pyrenean hills bareback; a beautiful, wild gypsy girl, never having enough nerve to go to the riding stables for a lesson.

Patrick's brother and building partner, Didier, was a small man, handsome and full of fun. His wife was Spanish, dark, motherly, and stunning. They lived in a nearby village that had a strong Mediterranean feel about it. Both brothers were hard- working and dedicated to their families.

The man writing on a clipboard and standing in front of me was obviously a debt collector. I knew the clipboard was there to try and make himself look important, and because he was nervous and slightly afraid. The only address he'd have for Patrick would be the village. That's all you needed here, the post lady knew everybody, and so to find Patrick he would have to ask around. That meant me, as I was usually the only person in the village.

"Patrick Viola?" I repeated, put my finger in my ear and looked up, as if I had to think about that one, "Never heard of him!"

"*You must have!* He lives in this village!" he said starting to shift from one foot to the other in annoyance, "He's a builder!"

"Oh! *That* Patrick!" I said and opened my eyes wide.

He looked towards me in greedy expectation, ready for directions, pen on clipboard. I stared over his right shoulder and scratched the top of my head, barbecuing him for a few more seconds then said absentmindedly:

"He moved to Spain six weeks ago."

I could feel three sets of ears straining from the phone box.

"Spain? *Spain?*" he said, "Are you sure? *Spain?*"

Marcel, Trio and the others had appeared at my side. With his head cocked to one side, Trio asked him:

"You deaf?"

He wrenched open the door of his car, slung his clipboard onto the back seat, climbed in, opened the driver's window and was about to say something mildly abusive when Marcel said:

"You drove in the wrong way, make sure you go out the right way this time, mon petit gars."

The debt collector put the car into gear, looked defiantly at us and sped off out of the village the wrong way.

My gang burst out laughing as the car disappeared passed the one-way sign.

"*Spain!* Patrick's gone to *Spain!*"

Trio said through tears of laughter:

"He's never even been out of the Aude!"

I eventually walked back to the house and started to work. They went off hunting.

After a while, started to think and worry about the mortgage again. What was I going to do? How was I going to support my family? I couldn't concentrate on work any more, too worried. Walked back home trying to think of an answer. I went straight into the veg patch and realised there was not much food to be had from the ground in winter. Walked out, closed the gate, wandered into the kitchen and sat down.

"You're back early," said Viv pouring me a cup of tea.

She had no idea what was happening in England, what with no telly or phone and the radio always on a music channel: for that I was grateful. She was rolling pastry out on the kitchen table to make a pie with the last of the veg. The kitchen smelt good; Viv was turning into a great cook. Keira was under the table eating bits of bread and jam. From outside came a honk from the school car, a door slammed and Victoria came tumbling into the house, taking a big leap into my arms. I swung her around, and then we all sat down for lunch.

As usual, lunch was fun. We laughed, ate, then all sat around talking about our day. I lied about mine.

After lunch, walked back to work. If I stayed at home Viv would know something was wrong. The day was clear-skied and sunny, I could see the Pyrenees in the distance. All the fields were empty, but the beautiful winter colours were everywhere. The small lane I walked along was silent except for the whistling birds. I had rarely seen a car or person on this lane, and the fresh air and views always lifted my spirits. No Woolfey today. Some days, I don't know why, he wouldn't follow me to work. He stayed in the barn, which was his home, and sulked. Today I felt like doing the same, my mood black and resentful. I felt useless and defenceless, hateful and murderous. The thought of losing my house, the house I was born in, dug into my chest, and with every step along the road the depression became deeper.

Then a loud snorting noise made me jump. I stopped and listened. More snorts coming from behind the hedgerow next to me. I peeped through the hedge and saw sanglier, loads of them! Marcel travelled miles to hunt these wild boar and through this hedge I could see a whole line of them, a complete family walking across his own farm!

'He'll never believe me!' I thought.

I crouched down trying not to disturb them then peeped through the hedge. I could see a massive boar leading the line, on his head were two big, pointed tusks that could easily kill a man. They walked in single file: mothers, sisters, brothers, tiny babies scurrying out of line, being told off and pushed back into position. I followed them from my side of the hedge for as long as I could without them seeing me. When the hedge came to an end, I lay flat down on the grass and watched them disappear one by one over a small hill, the last one, a baby, wiggling his tiny tail. He turned his head in my direction without a care in the world, full of curiosity and innocence, and then disappeared out of view. All that was left was their rich musky smell and footprints in the dusty field.

'There must have been at least twelve or thirteen sanglier there!' I thought, 'That boar has a big job protecting that lot, and keeping them fed, what with winter and the boss' gun. Not to mention Woolfey!'

The leading boar walked with his head up and tusks out, ready to take on any danger to protect his family. I knew his bravery would probably get him killed one day. His problems made mine look small.

'Tough bastard,' I thought, 'I'm not going to tell the boss about seeing him here; that boar had enough to worry about without me grassing him up.'

Got up, dusted myself down, stuck my chest out, and thought:

'And all I've got to do is feed three and a half people! Compared to what he up against, that's a doddle!'

The first thing to do was to get some money from the bank in London before they could see I was in trouble. Although I was completely broke, I knew that if I sounded desperate nobody would help. Had to think of a good reason to ask for money, something essential, something immediate. Arrived at the house, wandered around looking at all the work I had done, thinking:

'What do I need that I could *really* do without?'

The place was freezing cold. Pulled my coat tight and rubbed my hands together.

"This place could do with central heating!"

That was it! A loan for new central heating! Tell the bank manager I needed money for the plumber's bill. I had to be convincing; I had no cash to buy a ticket to London so would have to ask for the loan on the village phone whilst pretending I was sitting in a chateau, sipping premier cru with my feet up by the fire.

Went into town and changed my last hundred franc note into coins, drove back to the village and put all the coins into the phone box. It was an old fashioned call box; all the coins dropped into long glass tubes so you could see your money running out. Dialled the number and asked to speak to the bank manager.

"He's in a meeting, Sir. Can I get him to phone you back?" said a soft, female, cockney voice

"No, no, that's OK! I'll call back in an hour, if that's alright?" I said trying to sound cool and not let her hear my sinking disappointment or coins

"I'll ask his secretary," she said.

It felt like two hours later until she said:

"That's fine; he will be free in an hour."

'An hour to sweat,' I thought.

I went into my building site of a house and stomped around for an hour, practising my speech to the bank manager a hundred times. After an hour went back out to the call box, put the remainder of my coins in and dialled again.

"Yes, he's here, I'll put you through," said the same cockney voice

"Hallo sir, what can I do for you?" the bank manager said.

I went into my long, begging, lying plea for a new central heating system whilst watching the coins disappear down the tube.

"How much would you need?" his curt response

"£3,000." I choked, quickly explaining it was very cheap as the plumber was also doing the house next to mine, and I had to give him an answer today, "He wants the money in advance, in cash as he's not making much out of it."

"Difficult to answer so soon, paper work to do."

He was starting to sound indignant.

Had to soften him up; started telling him about the wonderful countryside we lived in and how he must visit us with his family. The coins were falling away. I reminded him that I had been a good customer for fifteen years whilst trying to sound cheerful and confident.

A glance down at the tubes, three coins left, he had to answer soon.

"I really must tell the plumber today or lose the deal, then it would cost me twice as much," I said

"It wouldn't be a problem if you lived here with an income; what *do* you do out there?"

It was time to get tough.

"Buy then renovate property," I exaggerated, "my budget did not include central heating. Living in the south west of France, I didn't think I would need it, but all the local estate agents say the French buyers will insist on having modern heating. I've had two other estimates, the cheapest of which was twice as much as the one from this man. He can do it cheaply because he would then be doing two at once," I repeated.

"Do you still own the house in London?"

"Yes," I said without letting on there was no equity in it.

There was one coin left, and then I would really be cut off.

"And you have to give the plumber the answer? Today?" he said.

My heart raced; I knew I was losing him by the way he said 'Today'. I had to take a chance:

"Yes, he's standing next to me," I lied, "why don't you ask him yourself?"

There was a moment's hesitation at the other end of the phone.

'Thank heavens for that! He doesn't speak French,' I thought, and as he was a snobby, pompous bastard, I knew he'd never admit it.

"No, there's no need for that," he said, "I could fax the paper work out to you. If you fill it in, then fax it straight back, I'll put the overdraft on the computer today."

I gave him furry boots' fax number which I had used twice before.

"That's very kind," I said and meant it, "don't forget my invitation to visit us," I said and didn't mean it, "bye!"

Just then, I realised an overdraft would cost a lot more than a loan.

The line went dead. He would think I put the receiver down but I still had it by my ear.

Filled in the faxed form, then sent it back. Gave furry boots a basket of tomatoes.

In France you could draw money out from your own cheque immediately, so drove into town, paid in one of my English cheques for three thousand pounds, knowing it could take a month to go through, and took out a thousand Francs. Went to the supermarket, bought loads of goodies for the kids, and good wine for me and Viv, took it all home and that night we had a party.

"What's this in aid of?" said Viv

"Central heating," I said raising my glass.

Over the previous months the artist had been inviting me over to his village for a beer. The bar there was barely furnished and stark. It was uncomfortable to stand there in the glare of the bar's light bulbs, so we used to sit in a corner. The patron gave us a small lamp to put on the table. I would treat myself to a packet of fags, and then we would gas about football and cricket, drinking cheap red wine 'til we were pissed.

This particular night I was telling him how Marcel and Evette had booked a coach trip to Germany as Marcel wanted to revisit the place where he had been held a prisoner of war. They had asked us to look after the farm while they were away. I was flattered and determined to do a good job. The money for the trip had come from the sale of a property Evette had inherited. The sale had gone through today so they were off next week. Marcel had given me a list of things to watch out for while he was away. I showed it to the artist.

"Why has Marcel written cats at the bottom?" I said

"No idea," he said.

I put the list back into my pocket and we went back to talking about football.

The bar had some holiday makers staying in the rooms they let out, there was obviously two of them stood at the far end of the bar now. They had walked through the front door half an hour ago, English, talking as if everybody else present was deaf. We did our best to ignore them, keeping our voices and heads down.

After a couple more glasses of wine, Neville was in full flow talking about the weekend's matches. I was only half listening when I heard it again.

Twice before I was sure the tall one had said it. The artist looked up at me, he carried on talking about football trying to keep my attention.

'So he heard it as well,' I thought.

I put my head back down, not listening to the artist any more, straining to catch every word coming from the bar to make sure I hadn't made a mistake. This time I heard it loud and clear. It was the big one with his back to me, talking to an older man, the older one just listening, not agreeing, just listening. I lifted my head. The artist looked at me then stopped talking.

The tall one was complaining he had been ripped off, had paid far too much. He had been in too much of a hurry, hadn't noticed all the things that were wrong and now it was going to cost him a fortune to put them right. It wasn't any of this that made my ears prick up in the first place, it was the name he kept using:

"Marcel Castignol, the thieving, little French peasant," he said, "sold me a pile of shit, fucking little liar. And his poxy wife, all smiles she was!"

I stood and wiped the cement dust off my coat, walked up to the bar and tapped big boy on the shoulder.

"Excuse me."

I saw the elder one back away as big boy turned around.

"What do you want?" he said, looking down at my dirty work clothes

"Who did you buy a house from?"

"What's it got to do with you?" he said, and started to turn away from me

"Tell me and you'll find out," I said and grinned.

He took his elbows off the bar, turned his body to face me, leant forward and said into my face:

"If you must know, a thieving bastard called Castignol!"

I grabbed his thick floppy neck, squeezed as hard as I could and pushed him backwards towards the wall. He was off balance and started to fall. I squeezed harder, lifted him by his Adam's apple and banged him up against the kitchen door, pulled him towards me not letting go of his neck, then banged his head backwards again. I must have done this five or six times and his face was now going a deep purple colour.

I had my face up close to him, telling him slowly he had made a mistake and he was going to say sorry.

The elder one stepped forward from the bar and said:

"Let him go, he's my son."

I hadn't taken my eyes off big boy. After one last squeeze, I opened my hand and he fell out. He staggered a few steps forward, lifted his arms onto the bar and slumped down, gasping. The artist appeared and said something to the elder one who turned around and said to me:

"I'm sorry."

"You had better have a word with your boy. Tell him to have more respect, 'cause if I hear him slagging off my friends again, next time I won't let go."

The artist walked passed me into the dark towards the front door. I went back to our table, picked up my fags, emptied my glass of wine and started to follow him. As I walked past the bar, big boy had his colour back and was scooping papers into his briefcase. Neither one of them said a word as I passed. Outside, shook the artists hand, got in my car and drove home.

Pulling up onto our grassy driveway I was glad to see the living room light still on. Opened the unlocked front door, went in and sat on the sofa next to Viv.

"You stink of cheap wine and cigarettes," she said not taking her eyes off her book

"How much did Marcel get for that house?" I asked her

"350,000 francs," she said.

'Good, twice as much as it's worth!' I thought, 'will tell Patrick Viola to put a bid in for the building work when he comes back from Spain.'

I started to chuckle.

"What's funny?" Viv said

"You," I said and kissed her on the lips.

Christmas was coming, and the three grand I had got from the bank was going. Victoria had the honour of being allowed to keep chickens on the Castignol's farm. It was while they were away that I noticed the fondness she had for the birds. After watering and weeding both vegetable patches, we went down to the farm to attend to the chickens. After we had fed them, watered them, and collected their eggs, she would go back into her hencoop and pick up her pet cockerel. She cradled him in her arms, he tucking his legs around her waist. Then she stroked his head and neck whilst singing him French nursery rhymes. He just sat there, a big, beautiful, multi-coloured bird nestling in my daughter's arms and adoring her. She would put him back down in the coop and then she and I would finish all the other jobs Marcel had left us.

Victoria had adopted the Castignols as her grand parents mainly because she saw them everyday and her real grandparents lived a long way off. Me and Viv used to watch her and Evette through our kitchen window tending the flowers in Marcel's vegetable patch. In the blazing sunlight Evette wore her big floppy hat, Victoria's small figure following her every step and wearing a smaller but identical version of the same hat. The vegetable patch glowed with colour from the flowers, floating pollen made the sight of the two of them hazy and surreal. They gathered up arm-fulls of flowers and herbs, then Evette would rest on a small bench that Marcel had made for her and listen to Victoria's non-stop chatter, nodding her head and agreeing.

Victoria also spent a lot of time with Marcel. Her main task was holding the chickens that were ready for the pot while Marcel thumped them on the head with that stick with the red ring around the top. After that she dug a skewer in behind their ears to let the blood out, then gutted and washed them. She had also learnt how to tell if they were suitable to eat or not; if there was any bad ones, Woolfey got them. Keira usually rolled around in the fluffy pile of plucked feathers while this was going on.

The two of them could spend whole days down at the farm, the only place that was forbidden was anywhere near the cows. Marcel had put goldfish in the cows water trough, so, of course, the girls would creep down there and lean over the fence to watch the fish. Walking home from work one day, I heard Marcel screaming and bellowing. I ran around the side of our house, stopped dead, ducked behind a tree and hid. Marcel was letting the girls have it; he had caught them looking over the cows' fence, they were getting the biggest telling-off of their lives. I wasn't going to interfere with that one! Crept back into the house and was glad to hear the radio playing very loud; Viv had seen and heard the rumpus and decided the girls were getting what they deserved. I realised how fond Marcel had become of them.

A week or so later outside work, I was cleaning a spade by a pile of sand. Marcel had come to join me.

"That cock of Victoria's wakes up at five and crows his head off," he said standing in front of me and shuffling his feet, "I never keep cocks. They're always trouble."

We changed the subject, talked about hunting, and then I went back inside to finish some plastering.

'The cock will have to go,' I thought.

We had been given the chicks by a friend, but we could not tell one sex from the other at that age, hence the cock. It was not going to be easy telling Victoria her cockerel was for the pot.

After work, I walked home dragging my feet and rehearsing how to put the news to her. Halfway home, I could hear the cock crowing.

'Bloody thing's got to go,' I thought.

That night as me and Victoria were collecting the eggs from her chickens, I started to tell her what Marcel had said about the cock.

"It starts to crow really early and wakes Marcel and Evette up. Then they can't go back to sleep," I said and felt like a wimp

"You mean the cock has to go in the pot daddy?" she said. My stomach turned over.

"Hmm, well, I suppose, err, well, we could…"

I would have gone on like this all night if Victoria hadn't stopped me.

"Come on then, but I'm not eating it!"

She went into her hen coop, picked up her beloved cockerel, carried him out and pushed him towards me saying:

"Hold him by the legs and tail then his neck will stick out"

She then disappeared into the barn. There was a deathly hush. The cockerel's head turned and looked at me, his eyes looked almost human.

'Where has she gone?' I thought.

The cockerel kept staring.

"Victoria, hurry up!" I shouted

She reappeared carrying Marcel's red ringed stick and walking in his same determined way.

"Hold him still daddy!" she said.

I saw her hand go up with that stick in it, closed my eyes, there was a swishing sound then:

"HOLD HIM STILL! You closed your eyes then moved as the stick came down. It made me miss: SO HOLD HIM STILL!"

Victoria was angry, I was unwilling, he was a beautiful cock.

This time I kept my eyes open and held the poor bird straight out with rigid arms. That stick was in the air again; swish, thump and the cock was dead, his head and neck swinging between my legs.

"Right, give him to me and I'll pluck and gut him; Mumma can have him for Sunday lunch," she said.

Walking home she talked endlessly, mainly telling me off.

'She's even beginning to sound like Marcel!' I thought, but I was pleased with her spoken English. Her pronunciation was perfect and she spoke without my cockney accent or her mum's Swedish one.

'It worked making her watch Mary Poppins five hundred times,' I thought.

The economic crisis in Britain emptied the house in London. The Dutch boys lost their jobs; there was no money left to finish the work on Kings Cross station, so they were laid off and left England, leaving me with a huge telephone bill. The agent gave me the good news then demanded more money to get new clients. As she had never filled her obligations over the past year (not inspecting the house every two months, passing all the tenancy problems on to me too late, taking no responsibility for her clients and giving me more headaches than they did) I realised that having an agent just gave you one more problem: them! I would have to get to London immediately and sort the house out myself. I used their last months' rent to buy an expensive plane ticket home. I knew it was imperative to get tenants quickly as I could use their deposit to pay the mortgage, but at least this time I wouldn't have to pay the agent's colossal commission.

Viv dropped me off at the airport. I took the flight to London. Arrived to a great cloud of doom and gloom, everybody saying that I would never find tenants for the house.

"The best thing to do was to sell it before interest rates took it away!" they said.

After living in the poorest part of rural France for over a year, I looked at their luxurious lives and thought:

'Perhaps they do need a good kick up the arse!'

Arrived at the house and opened the door. I felt strange, the place was exactly as we had left it; the furniture in the same place, not a mark on the paintwork, and nothing was scratched or damaged. The boys must have been working all the time and just come here to sleep. It was an odd feeling to be alone in the house; I wandered around dreaming about my past life here. The house made me feel free, safe and happy. I was born in this house, I had bought it from my parents then moved in. My children were born here, my roots were in the walls. As a child, front doors were never locked, friends and relatives wandered in and out at will. Life was simple; there was plenty of work to be had, you were paid on a Monday and broke by Thursday, parties at the weekend after watching or playing football, gas meters to save up in and the tally man to lie to. My family had lived in the streets around this house for centuries. Everybody rented their houses then, no mortgage to worry about; the only thing to save for was the train fare to Kent for one week's holiday, hop picking. We played football, marbles, go-karting, conkers, run-outs and rounders in the street outside the house.

Everybody said interest rates were going to take the house away from me; I was going to prove them wrong, no doubt.

In all the years I had spent wandering around different cities and countries, this house had always been there to catch me and, although the middle classes had moved in and most of my family and friends had been forced to move out, this house had always provided some shelter.

The thought of that sanglier came to mind.

Put an ad in The Evening Standard saying 'house to share' and waited for the deluge of phone calls I was sure I'd get.

After three days I'd had three enquiries; one form a married couple who wanted to share one room with their baby, one from an unemployed, socialist party worker who called me a "fucking capitalist bastard" when I turned her down, and one from a woman who said she had left her husband, needed somewhere to stay and then broke down in tears. It didn't take much persuading to get her to go back to her husband.

Put a new ad in the paper, lowered the rents by 20% and had the rooms filled in a few days. Made money a bigger problem as I was now getting less rent than I was a year ago, but at least I was, (as my Irish friend would say,) "still kicking the ball down the road."

'Time to relax and have a small celebration,' I thought, 'a couple of pints down the pub with some mates! They always congregate down our local after work.'

Our local pub was warm and nicotine coloured. It was a pub inhabited all week by men who then brought their wives along for a drink at the weekend. I put a white shirt on to show off my deep brown tan and marched through the pub door. Was greeted to a chorus of:

"Well look who it ain't!"

"Been away 'ave ya?"

"What d'ya want to drink?"

"Come and sit 'ere, boy!"

I did sit there, all night, drinking Guinness, telling stories and listening to tales only cockneys could tell.

"What d'you want to live abroad for? Everything you need is here!" asked one

"'Cos you're not there, you prick!" someone answered for me before I had time to move my mouth.

I thought to myself:

'If this lot spoke French, they would all live in the Aude.'

During the days I sat waiting for people to phone about the ad in the paper, I bought some paint and brushes to repaint the railings at the front of the house; black, shiny paint to make the white paint around the windows and the red bricks of the house all look clean and smart. The new, posh neighbours had renovated the fronts of their houses, the paint bright and fresh. I didn't want to upset them by letting my house get shabby. I covered the pavement around the railings so no paint dropped onto the flagstones, brushed the metal, rubbed down the rust, undercoated first, then started to paint the jet-black top coat on.

On the third day the job was nearly done. I was standing back from the railings, admiring my work, when a plump, middle-aged, balding man came walking along the pavement. I took a step towards the railings to let him pass but he walked directly towards me, stopped and said, in a well-spoken voice:

"Are you Mr Elusive, the owner of this house?"

"What do you mean 'Mr Elusive'?" I said nervously

"Don't you live in France or something? I know you inherited this house and you have lived here some time, but I have bought the house two doors away and I think things need sorting out," he said twitching.

He had pulled himself up to his full six foot but I still looked down on him. He was fat and flabby, ugly and effete, and he was trying to bully me. He looked like the sort of man who did that a lot. He was trying to make me angry, I didn't know why, but this thing in front of me with his staring eyes was obviously on a mission. I could feel the neighbours' curtains twitching. I thought:

'They've had a meeting, probably, at some stuffy diner party and decided they have got to know about me.'

They didn't like me renting the house out, no doubt thinking it lowered the tone of the area, so they would probably have invented stories about me from the pieces of information they could get from people who lived around here. They would build a picture up of some mysterious crook who was on the run, and no doubt fat boy here had volunteered to find out and sort everything to the neighbours' satisfaction. He had been waiting for his moment; I had been out here for three days and anticipation had made him nervous. I stopped staring at him and pulled myself together.

"Come in, I'll put the kettle on," said the spider to the fly.

I walked up the steps into the house, not looking back so that he would have to follow me. Walked into the kitchen, plugged the electric kettle in, turned, faced him and smiled.

"Need sorting out?" I said and smiled again

"Yes I'm the chairman of the local neighbourhood watch committee," he started.

'He's going to try and make whatever he's going to say sound official and not just gossip,' I thought.

"We want your address in France, or wherever it is you're hiding, then when you get tenants who are rowdy we can contact you and you can do something about it. We own our houses and we must be able to have some sort of control on who lives in the area. If you have tenants who are upsetting the house owners, they need evicting."

He stood with his back to the open kitchen door; I walked behind him and closed it, walked back to the sink, leaned on it, put my hands in my pockets and smiled at him. He knew what I was doing, but I could tell by his eyes he was going to brave it out. For some reason he oozed resentment and dislike, my instincts told me to be careful. I hadn't told the building society I had rented the house out, or the taxman about the rental income. This thing in front of me was vicious and smart enough to grass me up to both of them, and he looked as though he would enjoy doing it.

I pulled open one of the kitchen drawers, took out a pen and paper, wrote down my address and phone number in France, tore off the top sheet, then handed the pad to him and said:

"I understand completely. Give me your name and address and if we move, I'll write and tell you the phone number."

I kept my written address in my hand; he knew that in order to get it he would have to give me his and, as he wanted to return triumphant from his mission, I knew he would. He wrote it down, tore it off, then gave it to me defiantly; I gave him mine, put his in my pocket and thought:

'You're one for the future, my son! I can wait for you!'

He didn't wait for tea, just opened the kitchen door and walked out. I cleaned up outside, then went in and closed the door behind me.

The phone rang. I slumped down into a chair to answer it.

"Come over for a drink before you go back!"

It was the friend I had gone to France with. We had often spoken on the phone, and a few weeks ago he had been over to see the work I had completed on my house.

"You must have finished your house by now, do you think you could do mine next? Come round and we can talk about starting."

As we were completely broke, I phoned Viv straight away and told her the good news.

"When I get back I have some work," I laughed down the phone

"Good! Buy some English books for the children on your way home then," she ordered.

## CHAPTER FIVE

Since our first child, Christmas was a quite affair. This was no different, we would resents on Christmas Eve (Swedish), and ate Christmas Dinner on the 25th (English). In the part of France where we were now living there was no fuss about Christmas, in fact there was no sign of it until a few days before the 25th. The farmers around the area were poor and cut off from the big city. Christmas Eve they ate a mixture of seafoods in the evening before going to church for twelve o'clock mass. Christmas day, a few presents to open, there would be essential work to complete around the farm in the morning, a festive lunch, then back to work the next day. I can't say I ever really understood the people who became my friends and neighbours. The one thing you could not miss was the fact that they worked so hard; I never knew them to have a holiday, go to the beach for the day or walk in the mountains, most of them rarely left the area around their village.

The population was sparse; the local population in particular had reduced drastically over the last forty years. Most of the churches only held one mass every month. There were no cafés or bars in the villages around ours, though there might be a baker's or a post office, but generally the people bought their bread, fish, meat and veg from the vans that went from village to village. The dances and festivals were held in the village hall; every village had one and every village held a three-day dance once a year, the dates of which were staggered so they never overlapped. There was also bingo, religious festivals and sometimes just a fête as an excuse to eat and drink and dance. Everyone danced the same way: straight-backed, minimum contact, quick feet, a sort of tango-waltz.

Most people went to all the dances and fêtes in the villages around their area to show solidarity. There were two types at these fêtes: the dancers and the talkers. There was little or no drinking. Outside the hall a couple of stalls sold soft drinks and trinkets. Saturday night was disco night, a band sometimes but usually a DJ. The musicians in the bands were competent, but the singers were awful: sliding across the stage, singing songs that had nothing to do with the music. It could be a rock group pounding out guitar based heavy rhythm and blues, and then the singer would glide up to the microphone and start to cuddle it whilst preening himself and singing a soppy love song to himself. The audience rarely cared about this ego trip being performed on stage, they were all too busy talking. The evening always ended with a waltz.

Sunday night's accordion night, time for some good old fashioned dancing! The youngsters turned up for this as well, ready to dance, talk, and mix with the older crowd. It was very popular. Occasionally there was either bingo or a meal. Marcel and Evette went to all the local fêtes and talked to everyone, d. A lot of the people who did turn up travelled great distances, some booking themselves into hotels, some staying with friends, all drawn back through a mixture of homesickness and loyalty. I never saw anybody speak out of turn, there was never any fear for the children's safety no matter how long the night went on for, and the longer you stayed, the greater the night.

The region had been abused from the beginning of time, invaded, robbed and raped, it gave the people a fear of strangers. They weren't unkind, just distant and private. They never interfered with what we were doing and never asked any questions. They were very tough and independent: a local man was expected to be able to fix everything in the house as well most of the things on the farm. He could handle a cement mixer, a blow torch and a welding machine, repair all his own vehicles and build a house, run the farm and cope with all the emergencies that happened both there and in the house, and all the work he did was to a very high standard. The women worked hard and demanded respect. They were as versatile as their men around the farm though they dominated the house; that area was definitely their domain. All this, and raising children in the wilderness. The women looked after the children's homework, which there was plenty of. All the children had to work hard and learn, jthe school was as strict as the parents. Work had to be done. A man could be stupid, boring, miserable, rude, frivolous and drink too much: all these things would be forgiven, but not laziness. To keep respect you must be seen to work hard, or you were never respected, nor taken seriously. There were few acts of kindness and none of generosity. Money was short. You were expected to look after yourself and your family by working hard.

Honesty was also of the up most importance. There were no crimes committed by the local people; we rarely locked a door, took the cars keys out of the ignition, or feared for the children's safety. The local shops took cheques without asking for ID, credit was always available if you had no money and needed something. Sport played little part in their lives; it was considered a waste of energy. If you had that much energy to spare at the end of the day, you hadn't worked hard enough. It would have to a very special occasion for a woman to have a drink, even the men drank very little (except for the bread man). In fact, I never saw anybody drunk at the fêtes and fighting was certainly beyond their comprehension.

Because the population had dropped so swiftly, the people left behind developed a new way of behaving. They had to, being buried deep in the countryside. People think that in this situation they can hide; the opposite is the truth, you are on view to everybody's scrutiny. Do you keep your farm neat and tidy, what time you get up and go to bed, if you drink or not, go to church, how you dress, treat people, how hard you work, or don't, everything is on view to fewer people so is closely examined. You cannot get away with anything,

"Don't make friends with the people in this village. Three villages away is alright, then if you fall out you don't have to see them."

This advice from Marcel proved to be of great value, except for him of course. He could keep a balance with most people. Or so he thought.

You didn't turn up on someone's doorstep and expect to be invited in; you would have to be properly asked, time and date set, and then the occasion would be formal and correct. There had obviously been feuds over the years; we never heard about them but the fractions were obvious. The people involved ignored each other or talked to each other in strained voices.

All this suited me very well; having been surrounded by too many people for most of my life, it was a pleasure to be left alone in virtual isolation, no interference, everybody minding their own business. The local people tough and straight, but I knew where I stood with them and I was determined to win their respect. I knew they would never trust me enough to become a friend, even Marcel. That was fine with me.

We were desperately short of money; the loan from the bank had only lasted a few months, we were nearly skint again! To pay the bills I would have to start work on my friend Tom's house very soon. He was to come to France in a couple of weeks and I had to convince him that the work must start immediately without looking pushy and desperate as I knew if I did look poverty struck, he would lose confidence in me.

During a phone call from England I had been asked to take a boy on; there had been trouble with drugs, and his parents were worried and wanted to get him away. I knew the boy well and as he was a plumber told them to send him over. Broke or not, I hated what drugs were doing to some of the kids I knew at home and saying 'no' never entered my head. And if the wife asked, he was a plumber!

He arrived looking pale, thin, unable to put three words together, with a baseball cap pulled tightly over his eyes. He avoided us as much as he could during that first week. He would disappear into his room and stay there until we called him out to eat, which he did little of. It was obvious sleep was not easy, but he was very polite and never said no to work. He began helping me do some small building jobs for local people. He rarely spoke and only answered me in one or two words. He was shy with the customers and kept his head down as low as he could. I knew he had problems but sensed I had not been told the extent of them. He worked hard and asked for nothing; he was tall and handsome, and I reckoned if I could keep him straight and working hard, there was a chance he could get back into shape. It became doubly important to get Tom's work.

Tom arrived from England in good spirits, quite literally; he was pissed getting of the plane! Drove him to the gite he was to stay in for the next week or so while he decided what to do with his house. The place was a huge ruin. Although I was building our house, and had worked on small building jobs for an assorted group of English and French locals, this was a daunting prospect. Over the next few days I tried to look nonchalant, as if his house was not a problem for me, and implied to him I could only fit him in if we started immediately as I had so much work lined up. What really got me the job was the fact that he could not speak a word of French; talking to any other builder would be almost impossible for him as they spoke no English. He knew he had a week to tease and he was going to get his money's worth, as it was us who fed him and supplied his drink.

He kept me waiting until the second to last day. After changing his mind every couple of hours about the start date, he eventually decided that if we had time, could we start immediately? I went over his plans for the house once more then asked him for a cheque to buy the materials with.

"Don't you have an account at the builders yard?" he said

"Yes, but there's loads of other things to pay for," I said thinking about my electric bill

"If you send me the receipts I will send you a cheque," he said and grinned at me

"If you give me a cheque, I won't have to," I said and looked pissed off

"The cheque book's in the car, I'll write you one out later," he said and held his glass up.

We decided the house would have four bedrooms, two bathrooms, a kitchen, a dining room, two living rooms and a lounge. As well as all this, there were to be various rooms built and left empty until he could think of a use for them. He got on well with my apprentice and agreed to pay him weekly. All this was agreed over dozens of bottles of wine in the local bars. Although Robin, the boy, had joined us on the trips to the bars, he never drank, usually just sat at the table and said very little.

On the second night before he left, Tom said he wanted to go a trip to see the Pyrenees. I knew this meant the bars in the Pyrenees. We agreed to get to bed early so we could start at a reasonable hour Saturday. We left Tom at his gite; me and Robin drove back home for dinner. Robin said he was not hungry and went to his room as soon as we arrived home. Viv looked at me and shook her head. I waited for Robin to disappear, and then asked her what was the matter.

"That boy's a lot sicker than you think," she said

"He's been here a week, worked hard and been no trouble," I said defensively

"Trouble's your middle name," she said and put my dinner on the kitchen table.

My two girls hadn't seen much of me that week. Spent dinner listening to them telling me about their week at school. They both understood French and Victoria now spoke it. They loved the life here. Their blue eyes shone from their brown faces, all smiles and laughter, blond hair and grubby fingers; how I looked at them and loved them more then than I thought I could love anything.

Viv's belly was now leading her around the kitchen, a picture of domestic bliss. I was brought back to reality by Viv's voice,

"That boy must eat something," she said, wiping her hands on her apron

"He can eat after us, perhaps that's the way to get some food down him," I said with no real conviction.

We finished eating and had gone into the living to see Victoria's homework when there was a loud, a crashing noise from the bathroom. I looked up at Viv; she stood up and took Kiera into her arms, then she took Victoria's hand and told them they were going down to Mamie to have some dessert. They all walked out of the house just as another banging, thumping noise started from the along the hallway.

"What's that?" said Victoria.

Viv nudged her out of the door.

After they left, I ran up the hallway and into the bathroom; Robin was on the floor in a convulsive fit, foam bubbling from his mouth. He was curled into a ball, holding his stomach, a strange snorting noise coming from his nose. He started to thrash around knocking his head against the tiled wall. I pulled him away from the wall and grabbed him; he felt like a piece of twisted heavy wood, stiff and unbending, his eyes were open wide and gleaming. I realised this boy was a full-blown junkie about to have a weekend come down. The realisation frightened me.

Before I knew it the bathroom was covered in vomit and urine. Viv had been up once, took one look, and then said she they would spend the night in our house in the village. I'd had to sit on or hold down Rob whilst his comedown began and my strength ebbed away as the night went on. I couldn't leave, or go to sleep for fear of the damage he would do to himself and the house. I lay with my back against the bath and stopped him from bashing himself against the walls, the stink making me heave.

This carried on through the night. I fell asleep a couple of times but Robin's jerking woke me. Once or twice he was sick again. I cleaned up as much as I could keeping one foot on him.

I was sitting with my back against the wall watching the sun come up, the morning light bright and orange, wishing I could go out to my vegetable patch, when Robin started to relax slightly. I could see his body uncurling. He had been crunched up into a ball for hours and the tension was showing signs of leaving. I crawled over to him, saw his eyes close and hoped he would sleep. I started to wipe the mess off the front of my clothes, wondering how I was going to get him to bed, when I noticed his fists start to clench. He started to shake violently, his body loose and rubbery, then his limbs started to vibrate, his head knocked against the bath, and his lips turned blue. I stood up, took the biggest towels off the wall, put them over him and turned the bathroom heater on.

After about half an hour the vibrating turned to shivering, his eyes opened, he saw me and tried to grin but just looked awful. He said his first words that night:

"Robert, I'm cold. Help me."

I would have to clean him before I could get him warm. I turned the shower on, pulled his clothes off, grabbed him and held him under the hot water for as long as I could hold him up; then took him out, half carried and half pushed him into his bedroom, got him into bed, covered him up, put extra blankets over him, then sat on the edge of the bed waiting for him to go to sleep. The shivering stopped after a while, but his eyes kept opening and closing, and he began to fidget. Just as I thought he was asleep one limp would dart around and his body would jerk, then the covers came off him and I'd have to cover him up again. The time between these spasms grew longer and longer until finally I was sure he had gone to sleep. I bent over him and patted his head, until I could hear his breathing become regular.

"Rob mate, Rob, you can sleep now mate I'll see you in the morning, all right?"

I was almost whispering I just wanted him to know I was there so he didn't wake up and panic not realising where he was.

"It's all over."

I sat at the end of his bed for another hour. It was too late to sleep now so might as well see the job through, make sure the turkey was no longer cold.

When I knew for sure it was all over I went back into the bathroom to clean up before Viv got home. After everything was clean and tidy, I checked on Robin once more; he was sleeping like a top! Went back into the bathroom, showered, shaved, cleaned my teeth, then went into the kitchen, made a cup of tea, and waited for Tom to turn up.

Viv and the girls arrived first. I looked into the girls' eyes and realised you can't hide anything from children. They went out to play in the new sand pit I had just built for them. Viv started to cook and clean as if nothing had happened. I was grateful for that.

"Breakfast in ten minutes," she said.

I sat down and told her about my night.

"Eat this," she said, putting poached eggs in front of me, "you have got work to do. Don't worry about Robin I'll look after him until you get back."

She put her hand on my shoulder and said:

"Robert, no pub tonight. Let your friend find his own entertainment."

I ate my breakfast but felt rough. Tom arrived full of energy and laughs after his early night.

"You look like shit," he said, "early nights don't suit you! Come on, let's get going."

I dragged myself up off the chair, kissed the wife, hugged the kids and walked out the house, dreading the long day ahead.

We drove to the mountains through the sunny countryside and to my surprise I felt fine. Tom and I had always enjoyed each other's company as we shared the same sense of humour, but now, for the first time, our relationship had changed. He was now a customer, and no matter how hard he tried he was aware of the difference. He was the boss, he had the money, and as he was as tight as a duck's arse. I knew this would be a problem in the months ahead. I had no money no work and he held the purse strings. I knew he would give me the work it the price I would have to pay that was going to be a big cost. I had to keep him sweet, he enjoyed that bit; I hated it but had to suffer.

I managed to keep him out of the bars by telling him there was a better one in the next village and keeping to the small remote mountain roads. I managed to keep him distracted enough to set the cat in the direction of home, hoping to get rid of him somewhere before I feel asleep. Driving the car had been OK for the first few hours, but now I was flagging, a migraine had set in, the pressure of keeping Tom happy and the effects of the previous night were making my head thump.

"Stop in La Poutou," Tom ordered.

I had nearly made it home in one piece; I should have realised it was hopeless.

.

La Poutou was our local bar. It stood at a crossroads a few kilometres from my village and only ten minutes from the gite where Tom was staying. We were regulars.

The place was owned by a Parisian who employed an ex-jockey as his barman. His wife was obviously the victim of some sort of abuse, she was too timid and put down. Both her and the jockey were tiny so I reckoned they were brother and sister. I liked the jockey very much and spent hours listening to his tales about the track. By the look in his eyes, he missed it very much and I reckoned he would return to it one day. The bar was always empty, except for me and one or two locals, but the Parisian didn't care about this lack of business, he had another one going on in the shed at the rear of the bar, a weekend disco. The place was in complete contrast to the area surrounding it; the disco stood in the middle of the countryside, no houses within ten kilometres, and his disco was like something straight out of "Saturday Night Fever", all flashing lights and cigarette smoke. This was where all the local youngsters and wheeler-dealers met and imagined they were big city kids. It looked awful, but in truth was far more innocent then they liked to believe. From the crowd that turned up, I guessed the Parisian took a nice few bob over the weekends.

After avoiding any boozers for the last ten hours, I knew it was useless trying to keep Tom out of this one. I turned into the car park; we got out and went into the bar. The proprietor and the jockey greeted us with beers, obviously glad to have someone else to speak to. The bar owner spoke good English, he and Tom were soon chatting. I talked about football to the jockey. Although I enjoyed talking to him my eyes felt as heavy as lead and I desperately wanted to go home to bed.

Suddenly there was a loud shriek from their end of the bar; Tom had stood up and was clapping the bar owner on the back.

"There! At the bottom of the plans!" Tom was saying and pointing at a huge piece of paper the owner was holding up, "That's my company! We drew these plans! We know each other!"

It turned out the bar owner intended to open a hotel business in the Caribbean and had somehow commissioned Tom's company to draw up the plans. They were both flabbergasted at the coincidence of the whole thing and were obviously going to become good drinking chums for this night at least. That suited me; I had one more beer with the jockey then asked the bar owner if he would drive Tom home when they had finished drinking. By this time they were inseparable and I was waved aside. Put my coat on and was never so happy to leave a bar.

Went home, exhausted.

As I drove up to our house, I could see Robin and the girls playing in the garden in front of the garage. As the car pulled up Robin's head went down. The girls ran up and kissed me, I walked over to Rob smiled and said:

"All right mate?'

He looked up at me.

"Yeah, if you are" he said

"I'm fine," I said and nudged him.

We all laughed and walked towards Viv's cooking. The kitchen was full of the smells of home prepared food as usual. Viv grinned at me as I walked in.

"Sit down everybody," Viv said and looked at Robin.

He sat down and ate more than I expected him to; he even seemed to enjoy the food. The meal over, I felt very tired but knew there was still one job to do.

"Robin, would you give me a hand in the vegetable patch for a minute?" I asked

"Sure," he said and got up from the table.

With a great effort I managed to turn over some earth ready for winter potatoes and Robin helped. The job done I asked him to untie the bean canes that still stood after the summer. I sat down on an old wooden bench I had made to rest on. I didn't want to turn a chat into an interrogation, so thought better to give him a job, then he would have something to do while we talked.

"Rob, how do you feel?" I said

"Are you going to send me home?" he said

"No," I said, "but tell me what happens now?"

"I don't know. I have been taking hard drugs every weekend for the last three years. I haven't had a clean weekend in that time so last night was a complete shock to me. I'm sorry to cause this fuss, but please don't send me home."

He said this without turning around from undoing the string holding the canes together.

"You can't get drugs here son, so best you stay. How do you feel now though?"

"I'm beginning to feel a bit dodgy," he said and sat down.

I went into the house and told Viv she would have to spend one more night at our house in the village.

"The boy's still suffering," I said

"Keep him inside, I think he might try to run away; I would if I was him," she said and kissed me hard on the lips.

Although Robin did suffer and I didn't sleep much, there was no vomiting or fits, just pain and insomnia. I had to stay awake, Viv's last words frightened me. We played cards and I even dragged out some old board games. Red wine and cigarettes kept me going.

Three times during the night Robin had tried to go to sleep, but each time he reappeared from his bedroom after half an hour, wide awake. Dawn appeared. I persuaded him to drink some wine, then some more, and after he had gone through the best part of a bottle his eyes drooped. He looked very tired and pale.

'This time you'll sleep,' I thought.

He went to his room, I waited for what seemed like an hour but must have only been twenty minutes, went up to his door, opened it, peeped around the door, and saw him lying on his bed, fast asleep. I closed the door and can't remember anything else.

I woke up to the sound of the girls giggling outside my bedroom window, and Robin's voice singing them a cockney song about celery. I lay there, listening and hoping.

We started work on Tom's house the following Monday. I took Tom to the airport. He told me that one of the jobs he saw as a priority was the replacing of the staircase that had been damaged by fire. It was a beautiful thing that twisted upwards from the ground floor to the attic. I had never built anything like it before and told Tom I looked forward to the challenge. He carried on giving me a list of the things he wanted done, I realised if I didn't mention it again there would be no cheque, he was only nagging to waste the time 'til the plane took off.

"Cheque, Tom; I need a cheque to start," I said

"I know I know," he said and made no attempt to write one out.

He waited until his final call then wrote me out a cheque for half of what I was expecting. I drove back to start work cursing the fat drunk.

When I did get back to the house, Rob had started to clean out all the old junk and mess that had accumulated over the thirty years that the place had been empty. The house stood in the middle of a small village attached to the side of the church. It was the old presbytery, so bits of the inside were posh compared to the peasants' houses. It also meant the walls would be straighter, and the windows and doors well made. There was a small garden at the back of the house across a tiny tarmaced road. The garden was walled and me and Rob agreed that as the garden was a dump, we would put all our rubble there until we could find someone to take it away.

We spent the day shovelling the rubbish into a wheelbarrow and at the end of the day were pleased with our efforts. It was freezing cold but I was just glad to be grafting and getting paid.

Over the next few weeks we made good progress and got to know the villagers. Marcel's twin brother lived in the village. He looked far healthier than Marcel, the years in a German prison camp and ploughing those hills had aged Marcel compared to his twin. The villagers knew I was working black, but to be working and renovating one of their houses was more important to them. They understood I would find it impossible to join their complicated tax system and survive it, so as long as I feed my kids and lead a good life that was fine by them. Anyway, I was bringing in thousands of pounds of foreign revenue into their country and didn't intend to stay around to collect a pension, so actually, I was doing France a favour.

People started to drop in and look at the work we were doing. We got loads of free advice, and even started a baby sitting service. Some of the mums thought that, as we were in the village all day, they could drop their kids off when they were stuck. That was OK; their children were well behaved and no trouble at all.

Rob was looking fitter and putting weight on; Viv's cooking was doing the trick, along with all the exercise. I even managed to get him on a horse.

The mayor of the village often stopped by to inspect our progress although it took time for his wife to accept us. Eventually, during the days the temperature dropped below freezing, she began to bring us coffee and biscuits. The mayor's dad was a friendly old man who had a glint in his eye and was as strong as an ox,

"Look at this Rob," I said looking through the window at the Mayor's barn opposite Tom's house.

The old man was inside chopping wood with one hand, he held the wood with his free hand then lifted an enormous axe above his head with the other, brought it down and split the log cleanly in half. He had been doing this for half an hour.

"Bet he could eat ten weetabix!" said Rob.

I made some calculations for the wood we needed to build the staircase, and then ordered it from the sawmill. The owner of the mill said his wood came from the Pyrenees, then pointed up to the mountains at the exact place where the trees would be cut down. I asked him if he could cut out planks to the size I needed. He said yes, he would give me the centre plank of each tree to get the width, but I would have to wait.

When the planks arrived I still had no idea how to make a staircase.

The months went by quickly and Tom sent us money as long as I kept him on a short reign and kept nagging him; if I didn't, no money came. After dinner, I used to plan the next day's work and worry about how to do it. It was during one of these worrying session that the idea of how to rebuild the staircase came to me; if I could dismantle the old staircase piece by piece, use the old pieces as templates, cut out the shapes from the new wood, then reassemble the whole thing exactly as I had taken it apart, I should end up with a new staircase just like the old one.

Rob and I laid all the new planks of wood out, after clearing an area for a workshop. We did exactly as I had planned; the flat planks of wood were cut up then placed above our heads and to our great joy a staircase started to appear. It slowly climbed all the way to the top and replaced the old one. After the job was done I invited as many of the villagers in as I could. They all agreed it looked exactly like the old one, we had done a fine job, they didn't believe I could do it. We were now properly accepted. We may be strange folk, with odd building methods, but we worked hard and the house was taking shape. I felt like we were winning respect.

We celebrated by going to La Poutou that night and getting pissed. Rob's weekends were still difficult, but the effects of the drugs were slowly leaving his body, the cap was worn less and less, and he talked more and more.

"Look at this," said Rob.

We were at work having our first cup of tea of the day. I stood up and went across to the window he was looking out of.

"Is that a pig in the back of that truck?" I said

"It's the biggest fucking pig I've ever seen!" said Rob.

A truck had pulled up outside the house and parked in front of the barn. In the back of the truck was an enormous, fat, white, regal looking pig. His skin was gleaming in the sun and by the way he stuck his nose in the air and ignored the several faces looking at him through the bars of the lorry, he was used to being spoiled. He was obviously tame as he took all this transporting with an air of indifference. We went outside to have a look.

"Big pig," I said to the mayor

"It's for the village festival tomorrow, we feed one up every year. We kept him in a pen in the middle of the woods and fed him special food for a whole year. He looks delicious now!" the mayor said.

He started organizing the men from the village into two lines along the side of the truck.

"They're going to kill it here!" Rob said and looked worried

"In the barn by the look of it, but how do you kill something so big?" I said and started to follow the small crowd that stood by the lorry.

There were at least ten men helping to get the pig out of the back. It didn't object, this pig trusted people. The men were pulling it down a ramp by the ring in its nose. A couple of times the pig looked apprehensive and hesitated, though more from indignation than fear. Eventually it was teased into the barn and then things happened quickly. The pig was hoisted onto a long, low, wooden table and laid on its side. All the men lay across it putting all their weight down to hold it in position. Its head was pulled up exposing its neck. One of the old men of the village stepped forward with a big knife in his hand, held the pig by the nose and pulled his head up, lifted the knife with his other hand and cut a line around its throat from ear to ear. The line opened up into a huge gash as the pig lifted it's head and the cut gaped open. There was now a huge red crevice where his neck was. Blood gushed into a bucket strategically placed under the pig's head. The pig bellowed through the hole in his throat, the sound bubbling through the huge slash in its neck. The men pressed harder to keep the pig still; he was trying to get away from this attack and kept bellowing as the blood flowed into the bucket. The noise from his throat changed to a gurgling noise, then his body twitched. His eyes opened for the first time since his throat had been cut and looked directly into mine, small, round, shining eyes that looked human. His body gave a huge convulsive twitch and went limp. The men all stood up; they knew it was dead. They stood around for a bit then looked at the mayor. He started to attach a chain hanging down from the ceiling to its legs, then hoisted it up by a pulley attached to the roof beams of the barn. The pig was too heavy for the beam which started to creak and bend. They lowered the pig, and then attached the chain to two beams instead of one and this did the trick. A long, wooden, coffin-shaped box with no lid and chains diagonally across the top of it appeared. The box had hot water poured into it. The pig was then lowered into the box and the men started to wash and scrape the hair off it. They did this with the same concentration and gentleness Marcel had used with his geese. The chains that lay across and under the pig were used to turn it over, the bucket of blood disappeared into the mayor's house (black pudding), and we disappeared back to work.

A local electrician had joined us. I wanted the electrics to be done properly and this chap had been recommended by one of the local boys. He arrived one day and asked for the circuit plans, I gave them to him, he nodded and left, without saying a word. A week later he returned, 'The Great Silent One' as Rob called him. He came into the house, put his tools down and started work. All we got from him was the occasional nod.

A week later, after him saying perhaps ten words, he started to pack his tools away.

"I think he must be finished," said Rob and started to grin

"Well the Great Silent One will have to say something now,"

I said

But he didn't. He just left.

I got his bill in the post a week later.

After he had walked out the door Rob said:

"He's on something! I know all about that look, and that silence!"

He picked up a bag of cement, put it on his shoulder and walked up our new staircase.

'That bag weighs a hundred weight,' I thought, 'he picked it up as if it weighed ten pounds!' I grinned and went back plastering.

Viv had decided to start French lessons.

"I'm going to Mirepoix; they have a French class and it's free. It's supposed to be there to teach the local lady Arab population, which is quite numerous, to write French, but as the notice didn't specify what nationality exactly, I put my name down."

She said all this and looked slightly embarrassed.

"I think it's a great idea!" I said and gave her a nudge.

Over the next few months, whenever we went into Mirepoix for any reason, it became very apparent Viv was very popular with her fellow students. Whenever they saw her, or her them, that was it for half an hour. I would wait as patiently as I could as the foreign language class gossiped and giggled, exchanged goodies they had on them, and kissed and cuddled. Arab woman dressed in bright coloured exotic dresses, their dark faces, beautiful white smiles and piercing, gleaming eyes surrounding a tiny blond Swede whose grin matched theirs. Goodbyes lasted longer than hellos, waving and blowing kisses as they walked apart in different directions. Then Viv showed me the gifts and little bits of things her ladies had given her, things that glittered and smelt of spices, Viv's face smudged with yellow and glitter from her hellos and goodbyes.

"What do you ever give them?" I said

"Things," she answered

"Things? We don't have any things that are as fun as the things they give you,"

"They think the gifts I give them, are fun, my Dad sends them to me from Sweden, my friends think they're very exotic," she said and looked angry.

The thought of Arab ladies trying to open bottles of pickled fish and packets of hard bread made me giggle.

"I know what you're thinking, boring Sweden! But my ladies loved the glass and coloured wooden toys. We don't have any spices in Sweden, but I bet their husbands loved the schnapps I gave them," she said and looked unsure.

I grabbed her, squeezed her tight and kissed her hard.

"Get off you clown, everybody's looking!" she said and went red.

I squeezed her harder.

A few weeks later, me and Rob had arrived home from work early. Rob had gone straight into the vegetable patch to pick strawberries for the girls, and I had gone straight into the house following the smell of food. I heard a sound coming from the living room, one that I hadn't heard for a long time; I went in and saw Viv sitting on the sofa crying.

"What's the matter," I said surprised

"It's the Arab ladies!" she said.

I thought perhaps one had died, went to the sofa, sat next to her and put my arm around her. Rob walked in the door, saw Viv's tears and walked out again.

"The teacher is so rude to them, and because I'm white she thinks I share her prejudices. It's terrible! My friends will think I have lied to them if the teacher keeps behaving like this," she sobbed

"What does she do in the classroom to cause you such pain?" I said feeling sad.

"She tells the Arabs they're lazy and do not want to learn, that they should be more like me and work hard. Then she grins at me and carries on being rude to them. After the class today, some of my ladies ignored me, just walked right passed me! I don't know what to do! I hate the teacher and her prejudice but I can't stand up in the class and say so."

Living in a foreign country makes you more attached to the people who become friends, especially if they're as foreign as you. Viv didn't make friends easily but when she did, her loyalty was forever. I feared for the teacher.

I called out to Rob and lifted Viv up from the sofa. Rob came in with a bowl of strawberries; with his big smile and polite manner I knew he would make Viv feel better.

"Rob, help Viv with the dinner, I have to go out for an hour," I said and put my coat on

"An hour?" Viv said, wiping her eyes

"Need to see a man about building materials," I lied.

Viv and Rob disappeared into the kitchen; he was already making her laugh. I went over to the car, got in and started it up when Rob came out and over to me.

"What are you up to?" he said and leaned on the roof of the car

"Just call me Lawrence!" I laughed and drove away.

I drove around Mirepoix looking for a face I recognized. The town was very small so it didn't take long; I spotted the colour and sparkling dress first, stopped the car and walked towards a tall, round, Arab lady. She stopped when she recognized me then went to walk on; Arab ladies don't talk to men in the street. I walked in front of her turned around and said:

"I want to talk to the husbands of the women who go to school with my wife."

She didn't flinch, her face just looked into mine with defiance. She dropped her head and walked passed me; I followed three steps behind her. She strode into the Arab quarter of the town, stopped a small boy, pointed at me, said some words I didn't understand and sat down on a small bench by the side of a tatty house. I stood a few yards away, leaning against a wall.

After a few minutes, a group of Arab men came striding around the far corner. They looked surprised to see me, curious and friendly. The lady stood up and walked away, the men took me to a café they knew and asked me what the problem was. We were sitting around a big table with little cups of very black coffee in front of us.

I was nervous; they were all looking at me and I had to put my meaning across. I felt threatened, even a bit afraid, but my cockney character took over and I started to talk in clipped aggressive sentences.

"The teacher is an arsehole and she makes my wife very unhappy. Some of your wives have started to believe my wife thinks like the teacher. That has made her even sadder; she is so unhappy she cries. That makes me very angry. Your wives should not turn their backs on Viveka because of the teacher; she hates her!"

I picked up my cup and drank the coffee. The men picked up their cups and drank theirs. There was a long silence. They all looked at each other, then as if at a hidden signal, they all burst into laughter. Then they started to bellow with laughter.

I sat there feeling stupid and started to get up to leave.

"Please don't go," said the smallest one of them in perfect English, "Don't look so sad! Our women only go there because it pays! They can read and write in French perfectly well, but they get money to go to these classes. The longer they don't learn to write, the longer they can keep going and keep getting paid!"

"Why did they turn their backs on my wife?" I said and felt angry

"The teacher is very rude sometimes. The French people here think badly of the Arabs and it's hard to bear. All white faces seem to hate us at times. But it's strange to have to speak to you about this! I'm sorry about your wife; we have heard so much about her," he said then started to laugh again.

The oldest one among them stood up, came around to me, patted me on the back and gave me a packet of joss sticks.

"Take these home, light them, sit down and have a nice evening with your wife," he said and grinned.

Then I was surrounded by brown faces, laughing, slapping my back, winking, and saying 'have a good night'. They walked me to my car and told me they knew their wives would be sorry if Viv had been made sad. We stood around and smoked a cigarette then I drove to the travel agent.

I ordered three tickets to Sweden and gave them a cheque, gambling Viv's Dad would pay me later, they gave me the tickets; Barcelona, Paris, then onto Stockholm. Viv was home sick; she and the girls needed some safety.

I drove home and gave the tickets to Viv.

"All I have to do is shed a tear and I get tickets to Stockholm!"

I had bought two bottles of wine for me and Viv, and a good German beer for Rob. We had a great dinner with the girls, celebrating their coming trip to Sweden.

The meal and laughter over, the girls started to fall asleep. Me and Rob carried them up to their beds.

"I'm going to get an early night." Rob said

"Good!" I said, thinking of the joss sticks.

The next morning was Saturday, riding time for me and Victoria. She had started to ride a few months before and her progress was good. The club members had nicknamed her Victor and riding together was great fun. Our class consisted of a group of assorted children and grown ups. Different sized ponies and horses, different sized people, making us a team you wouldn't find in the Home Counties! But we thought we looked very professional. I still crammed in lessons on my own whenever I could but as the school had become very popular, Christine, the teacher, had less and less time.

"Robert! Heels down, back straight, look where you are going!"

She was shouting at me for the thousandth time. The small kids in the group seemed to get the position quickly; perhaps starting to ride at forty it will just take a little longer. I was certainly fitter with the work and the riding. I would just have to work harder.

The horse I rode only had vision in one eye, but the teacher insisted it made no difference to him even when jumping. I didn't care; I loved him and spent hours brushing and cleaning him. As he was so big, not many people could ride him and I started to resent anybody that did; I wanted him for myself and used to sulk when the teacher gave him to someone else to ride.

I had ridden in one competition and looked forward to the next. I wanted to improve on the four faults at the first fence. We had progressed to the stage where we were allowed to hack out. The farming land around the stable was owned by my neighbours. That meant we had thousands of acres to canter over, the mountains acting as a backdrop, the endless undulating fields and forest giving us beautiful scenery to ride through no matter the season. We rode for up to an hour and never saw a person, let alone a car.

Spring was here. Had just received some more money from Tom, our wages for the last few weeks. The sky was blue and the mountains looked great. Rob, me and Viv packed the car with clothes and a picnic, crammed everybody in and set off for the hills. Rob had started to feel a little awkward at times like this; I knew if he were to stay I would have to find some friends for him and had mentioned it to Viv.

"Not yet," she said and turned her back on me.

Although I worked with Rob all day, Viv was the one who could see into people, I was far too scatty for that. It would just take longer for Rob to get better I thought. Then thought no more about it. Maybe I should have done.

Tom had told me on the phone that he and his family were coming to live in France; they would rent the gite he had stayed in last time he was here, until his house was finished, then they would move to their house when it was finished and take up rural living.

The artist was over at our place with the hippie when I made this announcement to everyone; the hippie choked into his huge glass of wine, the artist looked delighted, Viv looked as if her head would spin off. They had all met Tom and his wife over the last few months and all agreed they were very pleasant, but hardly country folk.

"He will drink himself to death in a year; Andorra's only around the corner with its tax free whiskey, and his wife won't walk outside without pavement under her feet! Their daughter will never learn French, and they'll lean more and more on you Robert," said the artist looking at Viv.

'Thanks a fucking lot!' I thought. The artist knew Viv had said that Tom was a drunken waster; I knew too, but he was paying my wages.

The hippie liked the idea of having two upper-middle class friends, as he called them. I didn't dare tell him what Tom had said about him and his wife.

Rob leaned back in his chair and asked how old his daughter was.

"Too young!" I grinned back at him.

Viv opened a bottle of wine, and went very quite.

To change the mood, the artist stood up and said he was to have an exhibition in Castelnaudary in two weeks time. Castelnaudary is a pretty town on the Canal du Midi, a big place, big enough for a good show we all agreed, and as the artist was always completely broke, we stood and raised a glass to its success. Then I volunteered for Rob and me to help with the transport and hanging of the pictures. Neville handed us all invitations so we raised a few more glasses, then a few more, then the hippie stood up and announced he was going home. He staggered through the door, into his flower power bus, and they both staggered off. The artist stayed a while longer as he always did, then said his goodbyes, and as usual his beat up old car wouldn't start. We all pushed, then pulled, with no response from the wreck, so I towed him until the old banger spluttered into life. The tow rope released, me, Viv and Rob cheered. The artist disappeared into the dark, dark night, flashing his lights as he snaked along the long lanes that lead out of the farm.

The weeks before Viv left to visit her parents in Sweden were busy. Tom and his wife arrived, moved into the gite in their village, and Tom's wife made it very obvious she didn't like rural France, nor me renovation her house. Viv made it very plain that drinking trips with Tom would be heavily frowned upon, and Tom's daughter was defiantly never going to learn to speak French. Me and Rob worked hard and stayed out of everybody's way if, we could.

House martins were nesting in what was to be Tom's dining room. We tried to keep them out, but they could fly through the smallest gap with tiny pieces of mud in their beaks, making nests in the same place they had been doing for generations. Eventually, because they had started to injure themselves trying to get in, I left a window open, just enough for them to shoot through. I strung a clothes line across the room for them to rest on out of our way while we worked. We were astonished at how hard they worked to build their small mudded cups; we seemed to be working along side each other, both bird and man building a house. We felt a strange affiliation. Rob in particular took the birds to heart. He would sit and watch them at every opportunity. Eventually the window was opened wide so Rob could watch them flying across the fields swooping and diving to catch their food. Rob started to search out the places they alighted to collect the mud. He bought a pair of binoculars to study their movements, was always peering into their nests looking for the eggs.

Eventually the day came when there were four nests in the room. Rob had been up on the ladder at least ten times that morning to look at the birds. The females had started to sit in the nests so Rob was considered a pain.

"Put your cup down and come here," Rob said

I put my cup down and followed him through into the room where the birds were nesting. He walked across the room and stood under one of the nests. He made a soft clicking noise and instantly four chick's heads rose up to look at him over the nest. He clicked again and their heads rose higher. Just then one of the parents flew into the room over Rob's head perched on the side of the nest and fed the chicks. The parent flew off and the chicks' heads ducked down again,

"Great, ain't it?" said Rob and turned the cement mixer on.

I walked back to my tea, picked the cup up and turned to look back. Rob was shovelling sand into the mixer, the birds were flying around his head.

The village cats had become enemy number one. They sneaked around trying to swat the nestlings' parents out of the air as they flew in through the window. Rob swatted the cats with his shovel; they soon learned to stick to mice.

Tom made remarks about how the birds had better learn to fly soon as he wanted to start work on the dining room. I knew he only said this to give us the hump. He knew the birds had become our friends. One day he picked up a broom and started towards the nest saying he was gong to knock them off and lock the parents out. Rob spun round from the bricks he was about to pick up, grabbed the broom from Tom's hand, snapped it across his knee, threw the two pieces out of the door and then went back to the bricks.

"I'll get another broom for you, if you like," I said grinning at Tom.

He walked out of the door stepping over the two ends of his broom.

We worked five days a week and worked very hard. Rob had completed the plumbing throughout the whole house so Tom had got it cheap. But we were earning, so who cares!

Summer was here! Most Sundays we went to the beach. Rob, me, Viv and the girls played on the beach and swam in the sea until it got dark. Then we went back home, early to bed to get ready for the next week's work. Rob was now fit, brown and healthy. He talked freely and mixed with people much more easily. He was starting to raise his head and look over the horizon. How much longer he needed to stay with us depended on him now, as far as I was concerned he was ready to go home.

"You don't have to stay here Rob, not any more. It's a very quiet life, you must miss your mates," I said

"Do you think the drugs have gone," he said

"Yeah, I reckon. If not all of them then most. You look fit, boy, and ready to go," I said

"I don't want to go yet. I want to finish this house first, I just need some mates to go out with," he said

"What about the mayor's sons; there's five of them. They would gladly take you out one night," I said

"Yeah, I'm sure, but not yet," he said.

So we left it at that.

A few weeks before Viv and the girls were to leave on their trip, I took her out to dinner in Mirepoix. We had a great meal even though the restaurateur was obviously very drunk. He took people's orders swaying like a top, made bad, inoffensive jokes with everybody. This would have been very off putting, but as his wife cooking was delicious, nobody took offence except for one stuck-up English couple sat at a table in one of the corners. The restaurateur kept insisting I help him taste a new line of wine he was thinking of buying; I gladly agreed. To help him make his mind up, we had to go through several bottles. Eventually we agreed on one of the ones we had tasted several bottles ago if we could only remember which ones it was. For my services he insisted I sample his best brandies. It was during this sampling that Viv said:

"Rob needs to get out now; when I'm away take him out to meet friends. That way he might stay a little longer; it's too early for him to go back to the big city yet."

She then opened her bag and took out a box, opened it and showed me the inside: there were lots of small bottles of perfume. I opened one. It smelt very exotic.

"My Arab ladies gave them to me because I'm going on holiday," she said and opened a bottle.

She put some of the perfume on her neck and then put the box away. I thought:

'I hope it's the same stuff that was in those joss sticks!'

The meal over, we left, with my drunken mate pressing one last brandy into my hand. I gulped it down, said thanks, and Viv and I walked out to our car.

Driving over the bridge from the town that leads to our village, I was shocked to see a group of uniformed policeman holding their hands up and waving a torch at me; there were never any police here in the day, what were this lot doing here at midnight? Viv laughed and said:

"You're nicked!"

I stopped, opened the window and tried to look sober.

"Will you open your boot sir?" said the capped face looking at me.

I got out and opened the boot. He looked in at an assortment of kids buckets and spades.

"Thank you sir," he said.

I looked at his uniform and felt better, then got back into the car.

"How did you get away with that?" Viv chuckled

"It was customs, not the old bill. Perhaps I should show him your smuggled perfume!" I said and drove off.

The following morning I told Rob:

"No work today, we're going over to the artist's place to pick up some paintings, and then drive to Castelnaudary and hang them."

"Good! Your fat friend's house is being built too quick, and he is getting up my nose, the way he always keeps us waiting for our money. And every week we almost have to beg for it! He's a funny bloke, but a pain to work for," Rob said

"They can never stand to part with their money, especially not to a builder," I said, repeating words I had often thought.

We pulled up outside the artist's house, went in and Rob started to look at the paintings Neville had brought downstairs to go into the car.

"Can't make head nor tail of this lot!" Rob whispered to me.

We loaded them up and took them over to the gallery. The artist followed in his rust heap.

Hanging them was easy except the artist kept changing his mind:

"A little to the left. No, right! Up a bit… down a bit,"

He said all this in French in front of the gallery's young girl assistant, impressing her with his artistic eye above the incomprehension of the two thugs he had employed for the day,

who he was ordering and mucking about. As we weren't getting a penny, I leant forward and said to him with a big smile for the assistant:

"If you don't stop fucking about I'll hit you on the head with this picture in a minute!"

"Language, Robert, in front of this young lady!" he smirked

"She's French! She doesn't understand a word," I said cleverly

"I'm English and understand every word," the assistant said.

Rob fell of the ladder in gales of laughter, the artist went over to another painting and started to study it, I begged her pardon. She said:

"That picture you're holding's too far to the left."

After lunch, Neville said he was going back to his house to pick up two more paintings. I said I would go with him while Rob finished off. Besides, Rob and the pretty assistant had been talking.

'Make myself scarce,' I thought.

We got back to the artist's, collected the two paintings, had a cup of tea until we reckoned there had been enough time for Rob to make an impression, and then loaded up the paintings and set off again. Just before we got to Castelnaudary the artist rust bucket started to groan.

"Your oil light's on," I said

"It's always doing that," he said and shrugged.

We chatted for a few minutes then I noticed a tiny flame coming out of the small air vent at the side of the glove box.

"'Ere, Biggles, I think your car's on fire," I said and pointed at the dashboard.

"You're always so dramatic, old thing!" he answered just as a huge flame shot out of his vent and went over his shoulder.

He slammed his brakes on and we screeched to the side of the road jumping out as quickly as possible. He opened the bonnet flames shot out where the engine was.

"Get my paintings out of the back of the car!" he shouted at me.

I opened the back doors of his car grabbed the paintings, turned and ran after him. I caught him up as he disappeared into a clump of trees.

"You could have waited for me!" I said and put his paintings on the grass. Just then his car burst into flames

"We'll have to walk now," he said totally unconcerned about his flaming chariot.

I pointed at his car put my hand on my hip and said:

"Oh look! You're car's turned a beautiful sunset cerise colour!" and pouted my lips at him.

He picked up one of his paintings, nodded for me to pick up the other, turned his back on the flames, and started to trudge towards town.

When we arrived Rob and his new girlfriend were drinking tea and were not happy to see us. I finished hanging the pictures with Neville. We didn't see much of Rob that afternoon.

Lots of people turned up that night for the opening. Rob, Viv

and I had great fun getting dressed for the evening, a friend babysat; my girls were delighted to get rid of us for the night and have someone different to play with. We felt smart and happy to be going out. I told Viv about Rob's new friend and that added a bit of spice to the night. I was to be an English buyer and order a few stickers to be put on paintings that in theory I wanted to buy. In fact it was supposed to encourage people to buy something themselves. We wandered around looking at the paintings and chatting to potential customers. Rob disappeared towards the pretty English girl as soon as he saw her. Viv followed; the girl was going to get the once over.

I found the artist being catty to a Dutch man who lived locally and also painted for a living. There was a big arty community around Castelnaudary. Neville preferred talking about football rather then art; he hated this arty set. The Dutch man had invited himself to the exhibition as he was the group's leader.

"Neville your work has certainly matured over the last ten years," he was saying more to the people around him.

Neville's eyes had gone black.

"If you mean my painting has improved, it hasn't. I have just changed my style, but as you only vaguely understand one limited style yourself, I shall ignore your immature comments."

The Dutch man froze and started to turn on Neville, he was a huge bear of a man with violent red hair, and as Neville was only five foot two, this conversation was getting him into trouble.

The Dutch man was bearing down on Neville saying:

"You Englishman and your crude daubings! We Dutch are the great painters of Europe!"

The artist stood his ground but the Dutch man started to dwarf him. Just as he was bending down to put his face into Neville's, Rob's face appeared in between them both.

"I think it's time you went home, geezer!"

Rob was a tall lad, and very fit. The look on his face would have stopped a train. The Dutch man was a drinker who was big, but his body had never experienced exercise. Sweat appeared on his top lip. He looked sideways at me, I grinned and shook my head, trying to convey to him that if he started Rob would break him in half. The bear straightened up and went to the table of drinks, emptied a plastic beaker of white wine down his throat, and then walked out.

Neville broke the silence:

"Drinks anybody?"

Rob's new girlfriend was attached to his side, clinging to his arm. Viv came up behind me and said:

"There's not a lot wrong with your boy now."

"What about the girl," I answered

"She's beautiful, intelligent, she was kind to me and charming. She has a degree and is working here for a year to improve her French. Is that good enough for your boy?"

"Let's find Neville," I said and filled our glasses.

A dentist had a sticker put on one of the paintings and the artist had the cheque in his top pocket. Then he did the one thing all people do who sell their own stuff: talk too much. We had wandered over and were standing behind him listening to the bullshit he was coming out with.

"Yes, I have an exhibition going on in England at the moment actually, in a small town called Bath."

He was lying.

"Amazing!" said the man who had just bought the painting, "I'm going to Bath tomorrow! You must give me the address I can go and see it."

"Neville, that exhibition finished two weeks ago, you have got the dates wrong," I said leaning between them, I smiled at the dentist then pulled Neville away.

"You've got to learn to shut your trap when you've sold something," I whispered into his ear.

"Piss off!" he whispered back.

After the last of the guest had left, me, Viv, Neville, Rob and Abby (the new girlfriend) went for a drink in the bar opposite the gallery. Neville started to flirt with Abby, she put her arm through Rob's and nuzzled up to his side. I took the wife and the artist to a table in the corner and left the new couple to it.

We dropped Abby off at the place she was staying, a village house only a few minutes from us. Rob took her to the front door; I turned the car around so Viv couldn't stare.

After that we didn't see much of Rob in the evenings. Abby had managed to get her hands on a car and they were off most nights. It was always a joy to see her pull up in that old car, beaming and looking healthy and happy. They bounced off together looking for adventure and love.

After the girls had gone to bed and with no Rob, me, Viv and Woolfey started to sit outside on the warm evenings with a bottle of good red wine and two books. There was only one problem: mice! Viv hated them. They were always trying to get into the house, usually under the table we sat at, I had bought mouse traps that worked a treat. Every now and then a trap would go off, then bounce around as the mouse twitched in the last throws of life. When the flapping trap stopped, Woolfey would groan his way to his feet, lumber over to the trap, put one foot on the end of it, lean down, take the mouse head in his mouth and pull. When the mouse was released, he ambled back to where he had been lying, sat down and crunched his small snack. Every time the trap snapped, Woolfey had another snack.

There was the wild cats as well. Woolfey would go off into the night having heard a meeow from somewhere; we could hear his low, rough bark coming from miles off. Marcel had told me that wild cats must be killed.

"They're a danger to small children and vermin," he said, and as Woolfey was an expert at catching them he had hero status.

The building work was progressing and so was the stress. Tom had become a real pain with the money, and as he had nothing to do he followed us around the house scrutinising everything we did, or rather I did. He stayed out of Rob's way.

"Don't he get up your nose?" Rob asked during the morning tea break

"He pays the wages Rob, fuck him! How's the girl?"

"Great, she's real fun I laugh all the time I'm with her, I've never talked so much in my life. We're planning a trip to Spain together. Have you still got that tent I saw in the garage when I arrived in France?"

"Sure, man! It's all yours," I said grinning with glee, "how long are you going for?"

Rob looked down then up into my face.

"I don't know, maybe the whole summer. The gallery's shut until the autumn, if I don't go I might loose her," he stopped talking and dropped his head.

I realised he felt he was letting me down, he went on before I could speak.

"Do you mind, can you do without me? I hate to leave you here alone with that fat bastard."

"Rob, shut up! I can handle him! Go off with your girl, after the summer, come back. There will be tons of work left. Let's get out of here early and go and buy some maps."

I was going to miss him.

The day arrived to take Viv and the girls to Barcelona for their trip to Sweden. I hired a car as ours had taken a battering lately and I didn't want to wear it out; it was the only one we had and I had to be careful with it. We cruised down to Spain, hot and Mediterranean. We loved it, every inch of it: the smells, the mountains, the vines, the heat. I had booked a hotel in Barcelona where we were to stay the night, a real treat that we were really going to enjoy. The hotel was fine, and we decided to go out to see Barcelona and have a meal. We got back late and tired, but having had a fabulous time. Paella, the real one you can only get in Spain; my girls savoured every mouthful. We sat outside looking at the sea, the three of them heady with this adventure. The next morning, up early. Had them on the plane and away with no fuss. I drove back to our house a journey of four hours. Got home; Rob had lunch ready. He looked a bit down.

"What's the matter Robbo?"

"Abby's gone to England for five days. I miss her already,"

"When she gets back, you're both going straight to Spain. So, we'll get the camping gear together ready for the off. You won't have anytime to miss her,"

After lunch we went to work. We had decided to dig the hole for the septic tank, a big hole, but as it was hot and sunny, working outside was the favourite option.

We sweated and grafted for three days until the thing was dug. The Mayor had been out to watch and joke about mad dogs and English man.

"There's our fête at the weekend, don't miss it, will you?" he shouted at me over the wall that surrounded Tom's garden.

I poked my head out of the hole, and made an 'o' with my two front fingers. His head disappeared.

By the time the weekend arrived, the heat and hard work had knocked the pipe out of me but Rob was raring to get to the fête. He liked the mayor's sons and didn't want to let them down by not showing solidarity. Saturday night came, we got dressed and ready, then went down to the village. I phoned Viv which took five minutes; Rob phoned Abby which took half an hour.

"Let's go to La Poutou for one first!" I said
"Sure!" Rob said.

He looked good in his clean clothes, tanned and fit. No cap needed now, he was driving because he didn't drink at all now; Abby didn't like it.

Everybody seemed to have had the same idea; half the village was in La Poutou. There were a lot of people I recognised but Rob was the star. The girls almost fell over themselves trying to catch his eye; he looked good and obviously felt great.

After a little while we went up to the village and joined in the festivities. Rob disappeared into the village hall towards the music. I hung around for a bit, but the effects of the week's work had made me very tired. Went off to find Rob; he was with a crowd of youngsters and was the centre of attention.

"Rob, take me home, then you can come back and be with your friends," I shouted into his ear

"Sure!" he said with delight.

We were back at the house in fifteen minutes.

I got out of the car and said goodnight, Rob said

"I won't be late. It's Abby's birthday when she gets back and I want to go to Castelnaudary to get her a present,"

He went back to his party, I went indoors, opened a bottle of wine, went back outside and sat at the table me and Viv used. Woolfey came up and bashed my legs with his big tail. Poured a glass, lit a cigarette and felt rosy and warm. Ten minutes later my eyes started to close so went to bed.

## CHAPTER SIX

I woke to the sound of someone banging on the front door. I jumped up and walked straight into Rob's room: it was empty. My stomach dropped. Got to the front door, opened it; Marcel stood in front of me, his car behind him still ticking over. He turned and waved me into his car. I only had an old shirt, jeans and a pair of wellies on, I got in next to him.

"It's Robin," he said

"Where?" I said.

We got into his car; he drove off around the lane that coiled round the farm, down a long steep track that took us onto the main road and back towards the fête. I could see cars parked alone the grass verge and the red of a fire engine just before the track turned onto the road. As we pulled around the corner, I saw a group of men moving around. Some were leaning over a prostrate figure by the side of the road. My car was upside down in the field next to the road, a complete wreck.

Marcel stopped the car behind the fire engine. I jumped out and ran towards Rob's body. A helicopter was landing by the side of my car and two figures jumped out and started to run towards me. I ran as fast as I could to meet them at the same time as they reached Rob. He was lying on his back, his eyes were closed, his skin was grey-white, his shirt was pulled open. In the group of men surrounding him, I recognized our family doctor; he had obviously been attending Rob until the helicopter arrived. He looked up at me and shook his head. I looked down at him and felt my body freeze.

The doctor from the helicopter knelt down, opened his bag and took out two long spikes with tubes attached to the ends. He put one in each hand, lifted them, then plunged them towards Rob's chest. At the last fraction of a second, the one in his right hand stopped an inch above Rob's chest; the other went through his skin and into his lung. I stood and stared at all this, not really knowing what was going on.

I have no idea how much time passed, but eventually after the three doctors had been attending the lifeless body that I could only stare at, they decided to get Robin on to a stretcher. The Gendarmes, who had been standing around, moved forward and told the doctors they wanted a blood sample; the answer was an absolute no. The Gendarmes seemed to be insisting but the doctors formed a group around Robin and waved them away. They told the bearers to take Robin to the helicopter. I walked by the side expecting to go with them.

"Doctor, is he alive?" I said trying to keep my head together, and to sound calm and collected,

"Only just; when I arrived he was dead. If I had put the right resuscitation tube into his lung it might have killed him; his right lung is punctured and I would have filled him with air," the doctor said in good English.

"Will he live?" I asked

"I hope so," he said and looked at me. He took my arm and said, "Yes, I'm sure he will."

I felt tears well up in my eyes, my legs felt rubbery. I tried to stay in control. We had reached the helicopter and I started to get in.

"Not you, casualties only!" said a voice that shut the door on me.

I walked back to the road to say thank you to everybody who had helped. The Gendarmes started asking me questions about how the car got into the field; they had studied the skid marks and decided Rob was going too fast, had mistimed a bend, shot across the road into the ditch, hit the field, spun over once or twice and then the car had stopped on its roof. Rob had staggered out, walked to the edge of the field, fallen in the ditch and collapsed. They reckoned he lay there for several hours until a passing motorist noticed the car, got out of his car and found Rob. The local doctor came over and took me by the arm.

"Don't say anything to these people; we must stick together, Robert. Stupid bastards asking me to take a blood test from a boy who could be dying!"

He led me to Marcel's car, put me in the passenger seat and told Marcel to drive me home.

We drove home in silence. Marcel stopped outside our front door. I got out, said thanks and walked in, shutting the door behind me.

I went into the living room sat down on the sofa.

My head dropped into my hands again, then flopped down between my knees, again.

After a while I stood up, went to the kitchen and put the kettle on. I had to think. The first thing is, don't spoil Viv's holiday, not until I had to that is. The next, to tell Rob's parents. Then, where was I to get another car?

Walked down to the village and phoned England, told Rob's parents; they said they would drive straight over, through the tunnel, then down to me.

Phoned Tom and told him about Rob.

"I'll be over in ten minutes" he replied

'That reaction was too quick for him, he knew what I was going to say,' I thought.

Before I left the accident scene the doctor asked me to come and see in the afternoon, I had been wondering how I was going to get there, 'Tom can run me around for a bit' I thought

So, when Tom eventually arrived I asked him to drive me over to see the doctor,

"Sure," he said, his eyes saying something else.

"He wants to talk to me, I have no idea what about,"

"Sure, is it far?" he said

'Is it far?' I thought, 'why would I have a doctor that's a long way away? He's here for some other reason, I wondered why it took him so long to get arrive' he had kept me waiting an hour, stood by the telephone box.

He looked unsure.

I got in his car and said:

"Belpech,"

Leaving the village we were stopped by the Gendarmes.

They ordered me back to the site of Robert's crash. They put me in the back of their car, then, with Tom behind, we headed off. I doubted Tom would follow for long.

The thought of going back to the scene turned my stomach over. I started to fell nervous and afraid, I grabbed my feelings and shoved them down my boots. The gendarmes sitting ether side of me were trying to appear detached and hard.

I wondered why.

As we arrived at the field, it all looked very different. The cars, ambulances, helicopters and fire engines, had all gone, all that was there know was a car recovery lorry with the driver sat in his cab, by the side of the road. The police car stopped behind it. The three coppers got out, turned around and waited for me. I got out as slowly as I could, still trying to work out what they wanted. They led me over a ditch into the field. We walked through the scrub and weeds towards my upside down car. It had travelled about fifteen yards into the field, there were trough marks in different places where it had bounced and twisted. I noticed the window screen was broken where Rob must have smashed his head into it. The field was pasture, there was no crop damage or fences knocked down, so what was this all about?

All the doors of my car were wide open, including the boot. The coppers stood in front of me as if they expected me to say something; I picked some mud of the exhaust pipe. One of the coppers walked up to the back of the car with stiff defiant strides, looked at me with a knowing glint, then put his hand into the boot and lifted out a coat.

"Is this yours?" he said.

Thinking of Rob's drug habit I said:

"No."

The other two then started to pick out different things from the back and front of the car and point them at me; to every one of them I shook my head. I felt weak and sick, I wanted to sit down. I couldn't understand what they wanted from me. When we had arrived here, I had noticed painted signs on the road indicating tyre skid marks that Rob had made just before he crashed.

'But that's nothing to do with me,' I thought.

After they had taken most of the things out of the car and pointed them at me, then me shacking my head one of them started to lose his temper, he looked rigid and red. He took my elbow in his hand, squeezed it as hard as he could (which wasn't very hard as he was too little), turned me to face the boot and asked:

"What's all the yellow liquid?"

There was a gooey, yellow, globules sticky liquid stuck to different parts of the interior of the boot and back seat. Something had obviously been broken in the crash and emptied itself all over the inside of the car. I had no idea what modern drugs looked like, but looking at these coppers there must be one that was yellow and syrupy. I pulled my elbow out of the coppers hand stepped forward, bent down so that I could reach in to the back of the car, stretched forward and with my index finger scraped up some of the thick, yellow slime. Looked at it, smelt it, then very carefully and slowly licked it.

Then I offered the nearest copper my finger to lick; he backed away screwing his face up in disgust.

"EGG," I said and jabbed my finger at them.

I was taking some of Madame Castignol's eggs to the mayor in Plavilla last night, then forgot to give them to him.

They all looked defiantly at me. I wiped my finger on a muddy wheel, reached inside what was left of my car, took out a big piece of half-eaten chocolate the kids had dropped, and pointed it at the three of them.

"CHOCLATE," I beamed, then put it in my mouth.

They turned around and walked back towards their car.

I walked towards Tom's, who to my surprise had turned up.

One of the coppers walked over to me and asked if I wanted my car, otherwise the tow man would get rid of it. I turned around and looked at the wreck showing its belly to the sky. It was the first car I had bought from new. I had no great affection for it; it had started to fall apart from the first day I had it. There was a silence as I looked at the battered, useless wreck. The coppers, Tom, and the tow man were standing apart in the sun. I had no intention of keeping the thing, but I had seen this tow man leaning up against a gendarme's car in Belpech so guessed this was a police perk.

'It carried me and my family around safely for the last two years,' I thought.

I looked at the tow man, his eager face telling me he thought he was about to make a few easy shillings, so I walked back to my car, took out the spare wheel and jack, carried them over to Tom's car and put them in his boot. Turned around and waved at the tow man, letting him know it was all his. His face had dropped a fraction. I put my hand outwards, the copper took it. I looked him in the eye and said:

"Thanks."

Got into Tom's car, closed the door and said:

"Can we go now?"

He saw his chance; he started his car up, drove for a few minutes then started:

"Well, no work for the next few weeks then? I expect you'll need time to sort this lot out," he looked and sounded glad about this

"I'll be there at eight tomorrow mourning, *as usual*", I growled staring through the front window of his car.

'His wife will have another builder in if she gets a chance', I thought, 'there's been loads sniffing around, especially that hippie poet bastard and his wife'

The four of them had been very cosy lately. Tom's wife loved the way the hippie's wife sucked up to her. I knew they'd slip in the first chance they had. Tom saw this as a chance to please his wife.

"Don't be silly, you're in no state to work," he said trying to sound as if this was the last word

"You work and you're always in a fucking state! I will be at work tomorrow at eight o'clock," I said then leant back in my chair and closed my eyes.

I sat thinking:

'I bet that hippie shit is chatting away to Tom's wife right now, agreeing that he should help while I was away. Very cosy!'

But I wouldn't give him the chance.

Tom's car pulled up outside the doctor's house. I got out, leant down, put my head back in the car and said:

"Don't wait for me, I'll be hours. The doctor said he will take me home," I lied, "*See you* in the morning."

I slammed the car door shut.

Walked into the doctor's surgery and rang his bell. He came straight out, took me into his private office, sat me down and said:

"I want you to take these pills tonight, then come back and see me in three days."

He put a bottle of pills in my hand then continued:

"The Gendarmes won't leave it. They know Robin didn't have a seat belt on, they will prosecute him as soon as they can. They have asked the hospital for a blood test, which I know they won't get. But be careful of them Robert, we must stick together!"

I appreciated his concern so didn't tell him Rob didn't drink. I put the pills back on his desk and said:

"Could I have a lift home?"

"Sure," he said whilst quickly lifting his coat over his shoulder and slipping his arm through his sleeve.

We went out to his car. The sun was hot and everything looked too bright. I wanted it to be dark. We pulled away from the front of his house and drove up along the road that led to my village. The Gendarmerie was up on the left. As we drove past it I saw Marcel and his brother getting into a car that I didn't recognise. They didn't see me.

The gendarmes never nicked Rob.

I asked the doctor to stop at our village. I wanted to phone the hospital then walk home. The doctor stopped at the one-way sign. He leant back in his chair, turned, and looked at me, put his hand across to me, I shook it, he wished me luck, I didn't reply.

I got out, walked towards the phone box, opened the door and fell against it. I felt myself slip down the glass and drop onto my knees. I looked back over my shoulder hoping the doctor had left, I didn't want any more fuss. His car was gone. I stayed on my knees until the blood came back into my head then pulled myself back up to my feet. There was a stone seat by the barn next to my house so I went over to it, sat down, put my head back against the hay and waited.

After a while I stood up, went back over to the phone box and dialled the hospital. I asked about Rob, the girl put me through to intensive care. They asked me if I was a relative I told them Rob was my nephew.

"He is still unconscious," the voice said

"How bad is he?" I said and felt very hot

"It will take a long time, but he will recover. he was very lucky to be treated by the best anaesthetist we have, he could easily have died."

"Thanks," I said and put the phone down.

I left the phone box and started to walk home. I forced myself not to think of Rob, making myself notice the fields and wild flowers, listen to the bird song, walk and stretch and sniff the fresh hot air.

It didn't work. I felt like shit. The birds only reminded of Rob's house martins. Then I remembered Abby.

As I approached our house I recognised a flat backed lorry parked outside. Patrick and his brother were learning against the back of it smoking. As I approached, Patrick started to make a rollup. When I got to the lorry he handed it to me. I put it in my mouth and he lit it.

"You're working in Plavilla?" he said and took a large drag on his fag

"Yeah," I said and blew smoke through my nose

"We're are working in a village nearby, so we'll pick you up at eight tomorrow morning, take you to work, then bring you home at six, OK?"

He took one last puff off his butt, dropped it onto the gravel, stepped on it, and then got up into his lorry. Didier got up and into the other door. As they pulled away, Didier stuck his head out of his window and winked at me.

I got to work the next morning and started as soon as I could, before Tom's wife could arrive. Eventually she came up from the gite, saw me and walked straight back again.

'Fuck her!' I thought.

Tom arrived at about midday, 'ready to follow me around and nag' I thought,

Tom called me into the kitchen, I put down the tools I was working with, sure he was going to lay me off. I walked into the kitchen and saw him standing behind the table in the middle of the room, in front of him was a bottle of scotch, there were two empty glasses in the middle of the table, he reached forward picked up the bottle with his left hand, with his right palm he twisted the metal cap, then hit the side of it with his open hand, as I had seen him do so often, the top span to the top of the bottle, he lifted it off, held up a glass, poured whiskey into it, then he picked up the other one and did the same, he pointed this glass at me, I had been turning down his invitations to a drink for weeks know, I realised this was a invitation tinged with blackmail, but the thought of drinking turned my stomach over.

"Have a drink you look like you need it, come on," he said and bobbed the glass up and down,

I walked forwards took the glass and put it on the table,

"No I don't won't it," I said then continued,

"I'm going to give drink up for a bit, I'm feed up with it," I said and looked into his bloodshot eyes,

He looked straight back at me, lifted the glass to his lips, then hesitated, as if thinking he might do the same, the glass stayed still for a few seconds, I looked at his eyes, they narrowed, the glass tipped up, the whiskey disappeared from it into his open mouth, he put the glass down wiped his mouth picked up the other glass and did the same with that one, this time he banged the glass down, wiped his mouth, turned and walked out of the kitchen. I went back to work and wondered why I had said that, I thought of Toms act of defiance and laughed to myself, I didn't drink again for a year.

My head buzzed that day. I had to get things straight. My family must be fed; there were bills to pay. Rob would have to be forgotten; his parents must take over, they must look after themselves and him. I would help a bit, but if I lost this job I could lose everything. I had sympathy for them, but they hadn't told me Rob was a full on junkie when they should have done. I would shield my girls from what had happened; just tell them Rob had gone home.

I knew thinking all this was one thing, but feelings were another. I wanted to spend all day at the hospital, then care for Rob when he got out. But that would be stupid and could ruin me. I would have to deal with the emotional side of losing him later, but at the moment I had to ignore what I felt and keep everything going. I knew I would pay later, something would happen, but by then I would have things in hand, by then I could cope. I resolved to turn my back and let other people look after Rob. There was plenty of them; he had a big family and I knew they would make a big show of helping now it was too late. They would all gather round feeling magnanimous and mentally patting each other on the back for this good thing they were doing. Then, when Rob got well, they would let him go back to his old habits. Stopping a junkie's hard, visiting a boy in hospital, easy.

Patrick and his brother took me home from work as they said they would. Rob's parents arrived at about eight o'clock that night; they didn't seem interested in what happened, only in getting to the hospital to see him. I went with them to Carrcassonne, a journey of sixty minutes.

Rob was still in intensive care, unconscious. He was lying strapped to a bed with tubes coming out of various parts of this body. He twitched and tried to get up, hence the straps. I couldn't look at him; I suffer from claustrophobia so to look at some one tied down in a windowless ward made me panic. I had to get out. I waited until a doctor was found who could speak enough English to explain Rob's condition to his parents and then waited outside in the air.

Rob's parents would stay with me until they found accommodation near the hospital. I wanted to go home to bed but had to wait. I didn't have a car.

I did manage to see Rob once more before we left. I looked at him and tried to will his eyes open so the straps could be taken off. He just twitched.

Over the following week: Rob's parents found accommodation for themselves, Viv and the girls came home, Rob opened his eyes and Patrick took me to work every morning and brought me home every night. I steered Abby towards Rob's parents.

Viv did visit Rob once. That night I started to feel sorry for myself, Viv cleared everything away for the night, then said:

"It's no good both of us feeling sorry, I'm going to bed and so should you."

Eventually Rob and his parents went back to England. I never saw much of them, or Abby, again.

# CHAPTER SEVEN

Working at Tom's house gave me little time to finish my own; me Viv and the girls went there as often as we could and worked, or planed the next stage of building work. The garden had a terrible slope away from the house, so I had built a wall at the bottom of the garden, with the intention of filling it with soil untill the garden was level. The problem was where to get the earth from. Local people treasured their ground far too much to part with any of it, and we would need tons of it to fill in the space I had created. Eventually Viv asked the Mayor's secretary where we could get some. She told Viv that the council men cleared the ditches around all the roads so we should ask them. Ditch clearing only happened once or twice a year, and then you had to find the road they were working on. Viv had been going into the council depot whenever she had been passing. The Mayor's secretary had told Viv to ask for a Mr Vidal. Every time she went there and spoke to the man in the office, Mr Vidal was out working. Viv at the time was seven months pregnant with a belly like a big balloon so Mr Vidal on his return to the council yard was told that a heavily pregnant, blond lady was looking for him; we learnt later that this caused a great deal of laughter and mickey taking from his work mates.

During the time Viv was earth hunting we had been to see a friend in a local village, we were driving home when Viv suddenly screeched:
"Stop!"
I stopped and she jumped out and started running towards a lorry parked by a ditch. The lorry was full of workers going home for their lunch, the last of whom was being pulled aboard by his work mates. The sight of Viv galloping towards them with her long dress flowing around that belly brought looks of astonishment. They all looked towards one of their mates who looked very sheepish. Viv stopped at the back of the lorry and explained our need. Their faces broke into fits of laughter, all aimed at Mr Vidal; they slapped his back, and then told Viv the ribbing the poor man had been going through.

The earth was dropped of three days later, more than we needed. Their huge lorries pulled in and out of the village for most of the day, stopping at the side of our house then tipping a huge wedge of earth onto the road. By the end of the day we had a mountain to move. It would have to be moved one wheelbarrow-load at a time, through the spare piece of land at the side of our house, down a slope, over our small garden and into the space I had made. But I had a plan for this. All the men who had worked clearing the ditches around our village arrived up at our house to see how much earth I had and what I wanted it for. When they saw the small hill of soil they had given me and where it had to go, they scratched and shook their heads Mr Vidal squeezed my arm to see if I had enough muscle. He laughed and joked about mad Englishmen.

Viv brought out trays of coffee and buns, put them on a huge table. I thanked everyone for their work and the earth that would make our garden flat. I told Mr Vidal I would send him a photo of our baby when it was born; most of his coffee went down his shirt.

I had to go back into the house and make more coffee as Marcel, Trio, and Mr Regal had turned up. I had no doubt they were going to tell me how to transport the earth into my garden, and then how to get it flat and what to plant and how to do it, then walk away leaving me totally confused. When I went back outside, with the fresh coffee, the ditch clearers had left. I took the dinks over to the boys who were standing by a wall opposite the marie, the wall was for political posters, there were numbered sections one to six, each number had a rectangular space to put a poster on for a different party, the posters from the last election were still there or at least bits of them, there was to be a new election and thats what my gang were discussing. I had given out the coffee; the gossip was about to start when Marcel's famous ears fluttered.

"Someone's coming," he said and turned left.

We waited for a few seconds then a white open-backed van appeared from around the side of the graveyard. Rolled up posters were sticking out of the back of it. Election time was starting, this van was the first one to arrive.

A lively, young, male party worker jumped out of the van and started slapping gallons of paste onto his allotted space. He took one of his posters out of the back of his van, then walked back over to the wall, then he put the bottom of the poster up onto the wall and started to unroll it upwards, sticking it on as he went. As he was going through this much-practised procedure, he talked us through a party political broadcast for the fascist party. The unrolling revealed the words from last to first. We read them slowly as they came into view.

FRANCE LEAVE TO MADE BE SHOULD FORIGNERS ALL.

This was followed by a picture of Le Pen, the fascist leader. The young poster-sticker finished his work, stuck his thumb up at us, winked and jumped into his van. He drove off in a soft cloud of dust.

Marcel shuffled his feet; Trio and Mr Regal walked towards the telephone box, their shelter at times like this. Then Marcel joined them. I stood looking at the poster, more to tease them than anything else. I was reading the offending literature when it started to unstick itself and roll of the wall from top to bottom. Le Pen had obviously bought dodgy paste. Marcel and the other two had noticed the unrolling poster and came back to have a look. As the weight at the top of the poster became heavier than the bottom, it started to unroll quicker and quicker. At the same time we heard the poster van again; like many people did, the party worker had turned left at the one-way sign and had come back on himself. As he pulled up besides us, the poster flopped onto my feet. The party worker jumped out and raved at us saying that even if we did not agree with Le Pen's views, it was illegal to tear his posters down! He bent down at my feet, picked up the poster, walloped it back on the wall, and then started to paste the thing back up. We all stood and watched him while he re-stuck the poster working himself into a rage. In his fury he started a tirade against foreigners. He slapped more paste on this time than last, and then some more. He turned, looked at us, then whacked on a bit more, when he had the poster back up with enough paste on it to hold the wall up, he turned to us and said

"Come on! We're all good Frenchmen here, don't you agree there are too many foreigners in France today?"

Marcel pointed at me and said:
"Ask him."
I said with the strongest English accent I could muster:
"I can't say I entirely agree."

The party worker glared at us, picked up his pasting bucket put it in the back of his van and sped off.

We hadn't moved, just stood looking at that poster. Trio giggled, stepped forward, reached up to the top of the poster and pulled it. It started to roll off the wall again. This time I moved out of the way so I wouldn't get paste on my boots a second time. The last part detached itself from the wall and the poster flopped down onto the gravel. We waited a few seconds then, as everyone turned to walk away, Mr Regare stepped backwards onto the fallen poster and wiped his shoes on it.

The work on Tom's house had slowed down after the accident to Rob. I no longer needed Patrick to give me a lift. The week after the accident, a cream coloured Peugeot estate had pulled up outside Tom's house. A very obvious car dealer emerged from the driver's door, walked into the house and asked for me. He took me outside and showed me the car. It was perfect; it seated six. The price was cheap, compared to England, it would empty the bank of the savings I had managed since starting work. I asked the car salesman when I could have it.

"Now," he said and went into the Mayor's house.

He came out after a few minutes with one of the mayor's sons and told me he'd arranged a lift home. He gave me the keys to the Peugeot, left the address to send the cheque to and got in the mayor's son's car and they left.

I had a Car!

Drove straight home to show Viv and the girls.

Christmas was coming and Tom's house was almost finished. He had hassled me over the last few months to be finished before he left for his Christmas holiday. He followed me around from the moment I arrived to the moment I left, nagging and pushing. I had lost two stone in weight from being overworked and worried.

When Christmas came, his house was finished. Even his furniture was in place. All he had to do was fill his glass and flop in front of his telly. I went home with my last week's wages, exhausted but happy to be out of there. Determined that this Christmas I was going to have a bash.

Viv had the twenty forth, I had twenty fifth. I went out on Christmas eve and bought, cockles, winkles, shrimps, brown bread and vinegar. I went up to Mam Siprians farm and picked out a turkey, she said she would deliver that night. Fruit and veg, presents for the girls and something nice for Viv. I had crackers my sister had sent us and had even found a shop that sold streamers and hats. Christmas trees for the house were still something new here, but managed to find something like it.

Filled the car up whilst emptying my pockets. Drove home, prepared the veg, then put them in water, boiled the shelled fish, then put them in the fridge. I displayed the fruit as best I could using the bowls we had.

Mam Siprean arrived with the turkey ready to put in the oven.

She was a round Spanish looking lady, tall and brown, with blue eyes, she ran the turkey farm on her own, her three children still to young to help, what happened to the husband I never asked,. It was not unusual for ladies to be left alone here, the men worked hard and worried, not a recipe for a long life, in our area there were several woman with there children with no husband, some of the men had found it to hard and left, it was always the men who died or left or turned to the bottle, after they were gone the woman seemed to make a better job of it, certainly Mam Siprian was jolly enough and her turkeys were big and round, and delicious.

"come over tomorrow for a Christmas drink," Viv was asking her

"I would like to but there's so much to do," her tired reply

"Come over for a dance, bring the kid's, it will be fun," I said and winked at her

"Sounds good," she beamed, " I'll be here," then picked up her money and left.

Then it was time for the kids and the Swedish festivities. We did as Viv said, all singing Swedish songs, eating Swedish food, opening Swedish presents. All this sent over by Viv's Swedish parents. Viv's belly didn't stop her dancing with her girls and singing at the top of her voice. Ten o'clock and the girls were flagging, we cleared the room, and started getting the girls ready for bed

"can we have a good night story about Santa Clause," Victoria said and yawned at the same time;"

I sat at the end of Keiras bed making up a story, watching them squeezing there eyes together trying to force sleep to come, the sooner they sleep the sooner they can open there presents, but the more they tried the harder it became.

They lasted another hour, excitement keeping their dreams away, then in two seconds both of them were sound asleep.

I curled into a ball, tucked up to Keiras feet, and went off to join them.m

I could hear Viv voice in my ear,

"Wake up we have to get the dolls house," her sugery breath was saying,

I slipped of the bed and out of the girls bedroom, we crept out to the garage, then down the steps that led to the room beneath it. I turned the light on illuminating a dusty celler with a makeshift table in the middle of it, in one of the corners covered over with a cloth, was my pride and joy: For the last three months when the girls had gone to bed, I had been creeping down here, spending the evenings cutting out then sticking together a little house. Little bits of wood I brought home from work, wire and tiny bulbs I found in an electric shop, even miniature furniture Viv found in a junk shop. We carefully carried the little house up into the living room, put in on the floor, then I plugged the lights on. It glowed, a tiny bulb in each room illuminating the elfin furniture. We carefully carried it into the girls' room, then positioned it beside Victoria's bed. I went and got Keira's present, a collection of brightly coloured clothes she had asked for. Then bed for Viv and me.

We were up at the crack of dawn to put the turkey in the oven, set the table, open the beer and wine and prepare the music: Chas and Dave. This was going to be a cockney Christmas! I had invited loads of people around for pre-dinner drinks. What they didn't know was that it was going to be a knees up mother brown.

I covered the table with a big, fiery-red cloth, put out dishes filled with ice then put the sea food on top of that. There were bowls of brown bread and bottles of vinegar and loads of salt and pepper. The beer was German, except for some Guinness I had found. The wine was white from Limoux. Delicious! I covered the room in streamers and ribbon; the tree was small so I put it up on a table to make it look more festively impressive.

The first guests arrived and looked a bit put out. They weren't from London and seafood laid out like this was a bit of a shock. I put the good white wine in their hands, then went to meet the next lot. Soon the room was full, everybody eating, drinking and getting into the sprit. The French guests were shocked at eating so early but I told them seafood prepared the stomach for lunch. Once they were told lunch would not be destroyed, they dug in. Chas and Dave didn't go down too well with the la-di-da lot, but the German beer soon gave them enough confidence to join in the dancing. Looking around our big kitchen at the happy throng of muti nationals all trying to sing to Chas and Dave, and eat cockney food, made me chuckle with glee, I went over to the fridge were my wife was chatting to a Swedish friend she had just made through the bread man, Viv came from a tiny Village in Sweden, they were both astonised to find them selves's liveing just twenty Miles apart, I leant against the fridge and listened to there conversation,

"amazing, from that little place in the north of Sweden, now we live just a few minutes from each other, and only just meet," viv said for the tenth time

"amazing, from that tiny place in Sweden," her friend was repeating, " you must have gone to Skorna dancing on Saturday nights,"

"no, but do you remember the hot dog stand in Reabe,"

"not really, do you know, Inga or Bjorn and Breta, the family from Stowa,"

"never meet them, did you ever run into the gang from Dursland,"

"no,"

I leant of the fridge and asked Viv if she wonted to dance. She pushed her belie at me excused herself to her new friend and said to her self as we attempted to dance around her stomach, "how can she not know the gang from Dursland,"

The dance over Viv gave me a nudge and said our lunch would be ready soon so could I get rid of the guests. Everybody was having such a good time I couldn't say anything. I didn't have to; Victoria, having become very French in her habits, turned the music down and reminded everyone it was lunch time. Most left quite quickly, except furry boots and her husband, Steve. They were on good form, so we turned the turkey off and let them enjoy themselves for a bit longer.

Eventually, laughing and giggling, they left with their two young sons. I had the table reset with Viv's sparkling white china, the turkey out and the steaming veg in bowls within minutes. Viv, me and the girls sat down and were about to dig in when there was a tap at the window. I went over to the door and opened it; furry boots and Steve, the two boys and their dog stood there looking fed up.

"What's the matter?" I said looking at this bedraggled crowd

"The dog ate the turkey and the veg had boiled to a mush by the time we got home," said Steve.

Viv, who was standing behind me, pushed me out of the way, took the boys' hands and led them all in.

"Come on!" I winked at Steve.

Extra places were set, bottles of beer opened, hats placed on heads, then:

"Cheers! Happy Christmas!"

Crackers pulled, Chas and Dave turned up, we sung and danced until late.

The end of the year was coming. We had been in France nearly two years, the time had passed quickly. But time, for me, had slowed down, the next year would prove to be one of the best of my life.

Between Christmas and the New Year I had promised a tall, handsome, elderly gentleman who Viv had met in Mirepoix that I would repair his roof. He lived in a small village half an hour from ours. He had been to our house for tea and had charmed us all with his good looks and stories about his adventures around the world. His strong features, straight back, grey hair and moustache, all set off by his deep suntan, gave him an air of colonial majesty. The date to start work had to be squeezed in between Christmas and the New Year because he was over from England and he wanted to help me do the work. As he was seventy nine, I looked forward to this.

The day after boxing day I arrived at his house. He stood at the front door waiting for me, his moustache lighting up his face. He was wearing a blue overall and a pair of enormous boots.

"Cup of tea old son, before we start? Come in, the pot's on the kitchen table."

He was bouncing around like a teenager. He made me very happy.

"You bet, Reg! Got any biscuits?" I said and sat down.

Reg was a great talker, so I listened to him until the pot was empty.

"Come on, Reg, work time!" I said, getting up from the table to lead him to my car.

We took all my tools out then worked out a method of getting everything up onto the roof. Although Reg was extremely fit for a man of his age, I didn't want him up there. I realised, however, that keeping him off was not going to be easy; he was all ready shimmying up the ladder with a bucket in each hand. I rushed through the house, up the stairs and into the loft, it was full of dust and too low to stand up in. I had to bend down to reach the skylight.

'Perfect!' I thought.

Put my head out of the skylight window just as his head appeared over the edge of the roof.

"Lift the buckets onto the roof, go down and come up this way, Reg," I ordered.

He glanced sideways at me but did what he was told. The idea was to keep him off the ladder; he could pass me what I needed through the skylight.

For the next three days Reg's head and shoulders poked through that skylight all day long, except when he scampered down the stairs to carry up wood or tiles. I worked, he talked. He started by telling me he had five daughters, all living in Canada. He went through the list of grandchildren and great-grandchildren, but I couldn't keep track of who was who. He had been a keen athlete in his youth, a marathon runner and rower, then university and afterwards work in the oil business.

There was some confusion about the women in his life, there seemed to have been so many. After long descriptions of their beauty and elegance, the tears would well up in his eyes as he gave me a brief description of their demise. One tea break, I had to make him write them down in order, so I could follow his stories. There had only been two wives, one had borne his children then died of some awful disease whilst they lived in the Far East somewhere, and the second one was Swedish. That's how he got talking to Viv; he heard her speaking Swedish to the girls in a shop in Mirepoix. The old sod's tears appeared again as he related the story of his poor Swedish wife passing away. This time the death was a long torturous one; the other women were just passing ships in the night, that was how he described them.

After tea, back up the ladder, me to repair his roof, him to talk of his time in Egypt drilling for oil. There was a story about a drive in the fifties, from England to Cairo in his Austin Healy with his wife and daughters. Wherever he went, there always seemed to be woman and adventure. The days passed too quickly listening to Reg, the work just flowed by. He took me all over the world and I didn't leave that roof.

We had lunch in his small garden. He was a rotten cook, so I got Viv over to feed us. He loved that, flirted like mad with Viv, even though she was eight months pregnant. She loved it too. The three of us sat around his garden table, Reg telling Viv her food was the best in France and getting her to talk about her girls. If Victoria and Keira came with Viv, he was even happier, scooping the girls up into his arms and telling them they were beautiful. At the end of each day I hated leaving him there alone, but he didn't seemed to care. He stood on his door step and gave me a huge wave as I left, his big smile lifting the ends of his military moustache up.

The last day of the job went quickly. The roof looked neat and clean. I tested it by soaking it with water from a hosepipe; it was waterproof. Reg was still trying to get up onto the roof, I only managed to keep him off by telling him he would crack the new tiles. The work finally finished we cleaned up all the old tiles and the dust from the loft.

'I wish I could work every day with Reg' I was thinking as we went down stairs for a last cup of tea. There was a discreet, white envelope with my money in by the side of my teacup. Reg was leaving for England the following day so I had invited him over for diner that night. I asked Neville and his pretty girlfriend to come over as well.

'Let's see how the old devil handles this one!' I thought, 'I will put Viv on one side of him and Emma the other, he won't know which one way to turn!' (what a fool I am)

He arrived on time in his big old Citroen car, honking his hooter so my girls would run out and make a fuss of him. They did and so did we, Viv, Neville, and Emma. At the sight of Emma his eyes lit up, but Reg never missed a trick, Viv still got the first kiss and cuddle. I laughed, he was in his element!

Neville was soon charmed, Reg sat between the two women and entertained both of them at the same time, yet still managed to make them both feel special. He laughed and joked with me and Neville, ate heartly, and drank his share of wine.

He kept the evening alive with his stories about his adventures in the Middle East, yet managed to listen to everybody with keen interest, towards the end of the evening Keira fell asleep in his lap, Viv was pouring him another drink, Emma was telling him how wonderful she found his stories, Victoria was holding his hand in admiration, he carried Keira into bed, Victoria jumped into her bed and asked Reg for a story, he beamed with delight, sat at the bottom of her bed, then in a slow soft voice began a story about Queens and Goblins, I went back to the diner table, and finished my desert, eventually Reg reappeared stretching and yawning,

"one more for the road old things," he said settling next to Emma,

He then managed to glean a story from Neville, the artist is a shy talker, Reg with his worldliness put Neville at ease, he had the ability to stop anybody interrupting a good yarn with just his strength of character, I thought it strange that we were all listning to Neville but looking at Reg most of the time.

The story over, the night nearly done Neville and Emma said there goodbyes, I could see Reg hadn't finished yet so the three of us escorted the departing couple to there car.

"roll your sleeves up reg," I said out of the side of my mouth

Nevill and his pretty girlfriend were waving goodbye from there car windows 'optimistic I thought,'

Neville turned his car key, the engine turned over once, then died, this was yet another old car he had charmed out of some female art lover, he looked at me and grinned, I looked at Reg and smiled,

"I see," whispered Reg to Viv and rolled his sleeves up, we pushed Nevills car out of our driveway then along our narrow lane, Reg pushing harder than anybody, after a few yards the engine caught, spluttered, coughed, then the car glided off, the head lights came on, the car disappeared into a silver night, all we could see were the car lights illuminating the green lane, twisting and turning along the ridge then disappearing.

Reg turned around and walked back indoors, I looked at Viv she shrugged her shoulders and followed him.

I walked into the living room, Reg was sat, back at the dinning table his glass refilled, we sat down knowing he had something to say.

" On this trip home I hope to persuade a certain lady to marry me," he began, looking at the sofa, "she's much younger than me so it's not going to be easy, she's beautiful, and has independent means, I hope to persuade her to come and live out here, I'm getting no younger and feel I need a wife to look after me, I think it's a long shot, and so I will be gone for a long time,» he said all this in a conspiratal tone

he turned and looked at Viv,"

"yes,I will keep an eye on your house," she said, and patted his hand

"grand," he said, then stood up, "time to make tracks," then put his coat on, cuddled Viv goodbye, shook my hand and thanked me for the work and the fun we had had that week. Then he went out to his car and drove off into a hunters moon.

'Appropriate!' I thought, 'I miss him already.'

Through Neville I had meet a lady who wanted her house renovated. She was going off to the Alps for six months and hoped I could get her house ready to move into on her return. She lived locally with a retired English man, the house was her project over the next few years. I was very happy to get the work, so took Neville out to say thank you.

Viv's belly was almost ready to deliver. As always at this time of the pregnancy I became more nervous as she became calmer. She looked absolutely radiant, round and peachy, pink and delicious. Victoria and Keira were getting excited at the thought of another brother or sister. Viv had been told at the scan what sex the baby was.

I never liked to know, I always looked forward to the surprise, but from her kindness to me, I knew.

"All strong men have girls you know, I read it in an article in the Sunday papers. It's a fact!" she said and looked assured.

'That means I'm going to have another girl,' I thought, 'good old Viv!'

Marcel and Evette were curious about our families, they wanted to know if our parents were to come over for the birth. When I said no, they looked shocked. It was beyond their imaginings to miss the birth of any grandchild, or at least be involved somewhere during the birth. To them it was a family thing, to enjoy and celebrate. My family was too dispersed and involved in there own existence; Viv's parents had their own troubles. But to an old Mediterranean couple, this was a tragedy. The family was a major part of their life and there would never be separations. Marcel would rather die than lose his children. He had taught me how to be patient. I watched him pamper his daughter, picking strawberries on a Saturday, covering them in sugar, so they would be ready for her Sundays visit, then on her departure giving her a basket brimming with Evettes flowers and his vegetables, running backwards and forwards to her house, (which was an hour away,) to pick up her dog so that she and her husband could go away for the weekend, and always having love in his eyes when he looked at her. When she was ready to have her first baby, he would be there, telling her how wonderful she was, how clever to have such a beautiful child.

His sons he treated as friends; they were mates who worked together. Marcel had stopped showing his sons how to do things; they had sons of their own to show. Marcel nurtured his sons egos, praising their cleverness and listening to their ideas. When they arrived at the farm and obviously had to ventilate there thoughts Marcel generally took them into his vegetable patch, sat them down on Evettes bench, then worked around them, picking out weeds or watering some seeds, he let them drift off with there abstractions, never interrupting with unneeded advise. He let them sit there working out there projects for the future, airing there fears, frustrations, worries about children or spouses, while he pottered around them, just nodding his head, agreeing at their very clever schemes, encouraging them in what ever they wanted to do, looking concerned at there anxiety's, always being more willing to listen than talk, never interfering with there thoughts. Then easing them back into the world, encouraging and patting there self esteem.

Evette, loyal to her children and her husband, never flinched in her discipline and dedication to them. She like her husband both strong and reliable, always there for her children and grand children, safe and steady. What little time and love they had over they gave to us. I had never seen or felt such devotion from the background I came from. Marcel and Evette never confused sentimentality with love or loyalty. To them, giving love meant giving time and energy; millions of meaningless words meant nothing to them, you had to prove love by giving some of yourself.

Marcel had worked hard all his life to give his family a good home to be proud of. Evette helping her children with their homework after a hard day on the farm. All the children were educated and held good positions in the modern world. They were happy and well balanced. Marcel and Evettes reward was a loving family who surrounded them with affection. I was glad they were going to be around for us when Georgina was born.

One o'clock in the morning Viv woke me and said:
"I've started, the contractions are far apart so no need to rush."
She perfectly organised, her bag already packed, her cloths laid out pressed and ironed, the last piece of paperwork in her bulging handbag, money, passport, everything ready and waiting to go, me running around panicking, completely disorganised,
"Phone the baby sitter," Viv called from the bedroom,
I dialled the number, it rang about nine million times, then a voice answered
"That's you isn't it, Robert?"
"Can you come over? There's no rush!" I said, trying to sound calm,
"The contractions are still only once every fifteen minutes!"
What I really meant was: 'come now, please'.
" I'll drive straight over," said the yawning voice.
Viv's contractions went from every fifteen minutes to five, then four, then three, in a very short time, and still no friend;
I woke Victoria, then told her, she and Keira may be coming with us,
"So get dressed",
Keira can go in her pyjamas,

236 | *Robert Griffiths*

I carried Viv's things out to the car, then went back into her bedroom, she was kneeling on the floor in agony, I waited for the contraction to stop, then bent down picked her up, then helped her out to the car, opened the passenger door, and watched as she jerked her self on to the seat. I noticed she couldn't sit completely down.

The hospital was in Toulouse it would take us an hour to get there. The road would be bumpy and bendy, it twisted over the local hills, tight corners narrow and unkept. Looking at Viv I realised we might not make it to the hospital. I tried to remember the book I had read about delivering your own child. Victoria was in the back seat of the car now, I was wrapping Keira in a duvet and was about to plonk her next to Victoria when the baby sitter turned up.

She jumped out of her car, saw the situation was not as she imagined, walked over to me and lifted Keira out of my arms, she told Victoria to get out of the car, that done she said with a grin

"Off you go,"

I gingerly drove over our gravelled path, then slid along the lane towards Toulouse

In my rear view mirror I could see the baby sitter going back into the house carrying Keira, with Victoria in tow.

Viv had her arms straight down in a fixed position. She was holding herself off Georgina's head with her knuckles. We had to get to motorway, the road that would take us there was a country track-road, it was hilly and had tight turns which you could only negotiate slowly. There were bumps and lumps everywhere, I was trying to drive around them, this was made more difficult at night. Viv was being brave, not saying a word but in the moonlight I could see her face grimacing in agony.

I could feel the panic starting in my stomach; my mind began to race, my eyes bulge, that feeling of unbearable uselessness creeping over my body. This night, I cursed the isolation of our lives . I knew we wouldn't see another car, the houses were very few, hidden in darkness and mostly empty. I knew between the hospital and us there was little chance of help. I started to fear for Viv and Georgina, the distance between our house and the hospital became time and not distance, it's what I did in the time, how I handled it, I didn't won't this time, that was why I felt like panicking, I wonted to get out of the car and scream at God for letting me be so stupid. Viv's doctor had tried to pursuade us to have our baby induced at a arranged time, no we said a natural birth is better, why hadn't I thought of this scenario, what a prick I am. No help, just me, , I snatched a glance at Viv then wished I hadn't. I tried to talk, to make the time pass with out noticing it. But you can't talk a baby back.

Viv was now almost standing, crouched over, her head pressed against the car roof, her arms stretched out onto the dashboard, down wards. She was good at child birth, never asking for a pain killer at her previous births. She didn't complain about painful stitches, or suffer anything but happiness after each child. She breast feed both of them until the babies decided they didn't want suckling any more. I knew Viv would give birth on the side of the road without complaining.

'But what if there was a complication?' I thought, 'What if, like the others, Georgina would need forceps to get her out?'

I started to try and visualize a way to get the baby out using my hands; what if I can't do it, supposing I lost Viv, the doctors had a difficult time with Victoria, eventually cutting her out, I didn't even bring a knife, if the baby stuck, how would I get her out, my sweaty hands gripped the steering wheel tighter, what if Viv died, I must get Georgina out, then they will both be fine. How the fuck could I do it. Just then a hollow appeared at the edge of the road, I swerved to avoid it, Viv yelled in pain. I couldn't help her, my head bounded with her pain. Sweat dripped of my forehead onto the steering wheel.

'Please God, don't take my wife and baby! Not like this, not here, not now!' I begged

I would have said or done anything at that moment, just to be in the white clean hospital, full of doctors and equipment, bright lights and disinfectant. I promised God my soul if he let them live, I threatened to give it to the Devil if they died.

"Darling, I think you will have to stop," Viv said through gritted teeth

"Just a little while longer, there's a barn a few miles away, with hay, it won't take long, I promise" I said and felt my heart lighten as the clouds cleared and the bright white light of the moon illuminated the road ahead.

'Half an hour and we will be on the motorway! Just half an hour , Georgina please wait, then flat tarmac and speed, just this fucking road to get passed first' I thought.

"Viv, sit down a bit it might help," I said,

"I can't, really, I can't," Viv said and looked across at me.

In the moonlight she still looked beautiful, even at times like this.

"Stop worrying everything will be fine," she said and tried to look serine.

I felt so desperate at the thought of loosing her, tears kept filling my eyes.

'Fuck this Griffiths! Control yourself or you won't cope, you idiot, think of what you have got to do and control yourself.

Although I knew every inch of this road I still watched the kilometres tick over, willing the little figures to go around quicker, Viv was sweating so much the windows started to steam up, her panting became louder, her limbs stiffer, she let out a long low moan; I braked and eased the car to the side of the road

"What is it?" I said taking her hand and holding it.

"The pain, this time it's so much more, it didn't feel like this the times before. Robert, there's something wrong! The pain's different!" Viv said this while her face turned a creamy white colour.

I let go of her hand, put the car in gear, drove back onto the road, and said

"Sit on the edge of your seat and lean back. This time, do what I say, please sweetheart," I said and accelerated up to a speed I hoped to be able to handle.

Viv started to breath heavily, then started panting. I looked across at her. Sweat covered her forehead and her eyes were tight shut and scrawled up. She had lifted her legs onto the dashboard and started to have another contraction.

"Sit upright, Viv! Sit upright!" I shouted at her.

She didn't hear me.

'There's something wrong! I mustn't stop until she starts to give birth. I must get as near to the hospital as possible, then cope with whatever the problem is.'

The lights of the motorway shone in the distance

'Just get that far then look for help. Just ten more minutes and we will be safe!' I was saying to myself.

"Viv hold on, nearly there!"

I didn't see the lump in the road until it was too late, the left front wheel hit it, then the car thudded up and down lifting Viv in the air then forcing her down onto her seat, she screamed in pain then flopped forwards onto her knees, her head banged against the dashboard. I didn't stop, I had to get help. The light of the tool booth was illuminating the sky in front of me, silhouetting the last hill we had to climb. I accelerated gingerly, Viv started to moan and sway but not moving her position. I just needed two more minutes, then the bumping would stop.

"Robert please stop, please!"

"One more minute, Viv, and we will be safe. I lied!"

I glanced across at her in the darkness and thought I saw blood on the floor between her legs, a pool of it. I looked away and tried lift us over this endless hill.

I couldn't look at Viv, I wouldn't until we were going down the other side, and I could see the tollbooth. I could feel her body slump, I didn't have to turn my head and see it. I pushed the accelerator down harder, the car jumped forward, I knew Viv had passed out, I could feel the silence and the limp body on the floor of the drivers seat. I was not going to stop until I reached the toll booth. The car slid over the top of the hill, light were drawing us towards them, going down instead of up changed my feelings, the car was driving itself, it had become deafingly silent. I turned to look at Viv, she wasn't moving. I whispered her name;

"sweat heart were here, the motorway, Viv answer me,"

this time I did stop the car, got out and went round to the passenger side, opened the door slowly, put my hand inside and lifted Viv's head, it felt cold and clammy, her hair stuck to my hand, I put my head next to hers and kissed the sweat away,

"darling please, please, I'm sorry" I pleaded

she stirred then turned her head towards me. Her hair was stuck to her forehead and covered in sweat. Her eyes looked bloodshot and filled with water. She put her hand on top of mine patted it and smiled at me. I squeezed her hand tight and smiled back;

"Keep going we must get Georgina to the hospital," she said .

I stood up and looked towards the lighted tollbooth, it looked like the gates of heaven to me. I walked around the car to the drivers seat got in, started the engine and drove towards that brilliance. Viv immediately went back to resting on her knuckles. I drove up to the automatic ticket machine. The ticket came out, I grabbed it and then pressed the accelerator down as far as it would go. The motorway was deserted. I had hoped there would be a few cars, but at this time in the morning traffic was non-existent. Ten minutes, then we would turn off the motorway and towards the centre of Toulouse. From there the hospital was only fifteen minutes. I had practised this route several times, I wonted to be familiar with the roads, I didn't drive in cities anymore, there was many streets to remember, I tried to memorise it now, but I had lost confidence and couldn't remember which way to go.

'I'm going to get fucking lost in the town!' I thought.

We reached the pay booth, I pulled up as gently as I could. The window opened and a friendly smiling face peered out. A dark, handsome, middle-aged man was about to say 'Bonjour' but his lips stopped as he saw Viv straining against the roof of the car.

"The baby's coming!" I said and put my shoulders and the palms of my hands up

"Go, go! Quick! Quick!" he said whilst waving his hands towards Toulouse.

The barrier opened and I drove through. He didn't asked for any money.

I drove by instinct.

I thought: 'Don't think about it. You must know the way; you have practised it *four times*!'

A police car pulled in front of me and sounded his alarm whilst slowly bringing me to a stop, a tall stockie uniformed Gerdarm jumped out. I was very happy to see them, I knew they would forget any minor driving offence once they saw Viv.

The policeman ran towards us, stopped at my window and ducked down.

"Which hospital are you going to?" he said and looked at Viv.

She was creased in agony and pushing her hands as hard as she could against the dashboard. I turned back to tell the policeman which hospital, I noticed his expression changed

"Follow us!" he said then bolted back to his car.

I thought 'The man in the tollbooth must have contacted them,'

We were at the hospital in less then five minutes. With their siren on, they took a route I had never found, a short cut.

Outside the hospital, I parked on the pavement, jumped out of the car, ran around to Viv's door, opened it and helped her out. She couldn't walk by herself. A nurse appeared pushing a wheelchair and scooped Viv into it. I turned and shook the policeman's hand; he took it and me to the door of the hospital and ushered me inside. We were in the lift, and then out and into the delivery room in seconds. There was our doctor putting gloves on and ushering a rounded lady off the delivery bed. The police had organised this whilst leading us here. Viv was put on the bed, in place of the other pregnant woman, who was being told there was a more urgent delivery. I went into my usual position at Viv's left side. The doctor and nurses took their places automatically. A quick examination told them the baby was nearly out. They didn't bother to undress her

At the next contraction Georgina was born.

A nurse carried Georgina to a table at the side of Viv's bed and started to clean her. Then the after-birth and a couple of stitches, that finished, Viv got off the bed and wobbled towards the door.

"Where are you going?" I said astonished

"Toilet," she said over her shoulder

"Back on that bed," I said and looked at the faces of the nurses.

They jumped forwards and put Viv back on the delivery bed, laughing at her toughness.

Viv was undressed, cleaned, put in a white nightdress, then they put her and Georgina on a trolley, I was told to take them to a room along the corridor.

The nurse explained;

"Full moons are always busy!"

Then she shut the door behind me as the woman who was shovelled out as Viv came in was brought back in again. I took Viv along to the room the nurse had sent me to, opened the door and pushed the trolley inside. The room had two beds, both beds filled with post-pregnant ladies. I looked for the third bed in vain, went back outside and asked a passing nurse if I had the correct room.

"yes," she said "We're very busy. I'll get you a mattress for the time being," then walked up the hallway.

I returned to the room and told Viv she would have to sleep on a mattress between the two beds. I felt like screaming. Viv would have to squeeze in between two beds in a room only really big enough for one.

I started to get angry.

Viv put our new baby in the spare cot by the toilet door, then told me to watch her. She took the mattress off the incoming nurse and made herself a bed in the space between the other two ladies. I took my baby out of her cot and would have taken her home if Viv hadn't grabbed Georgina and told *me* to go home. She got down onto her bed with her new baby, they both slid under the covers, I got down on my knees and kissed both heads, kissed Vivs eyes, and told her she was a genius, I stroked her head until she feel asleep, Georgina stared at me in wide eyed amazement, I stood up and bowed to Vivs two neighbours, then walked out into the corridor; A pretty dark nurse asked me were the baby was, I explained she was in bed with her mother and if she didn't wont to risk her life she should leave it like that.

I drove home, I felt light headed and grateful, I thought it must feel like this when you win the pools, Georgina was safe and warm, if a little cramped. Viv was wrapped up and fast asleep, and alive, warm with our baby in her arms.

I thought of the woman I had named Georgina after: a tall, beautiful lady, whom I had loved. She was funny and posh, clever and kind. She was an actress who could charm people and make them laugh. I wondered where she was and felt guilty I didn't know.

The sun was shining, the mountains looked big and green, with snow whitening the tops . The winter colours of the trees and hedges, bushes and fields blended together perfectly.

I travelled back toward the children on the same road. The darkness had gone, I was pleased to be out of the city and in open isolated countryside again. I stopped the car, got out, went round to the passenger's door, opened it, bent down and looked at the floor where Viv had been crouched. There was a pool of water. I closed the door, walked across the lane and into a wild flower filled pasture that had been left to fallow, sat down on a cold stone and thanked God for answering my prayers.

We still lived on the farm; our house in the village was nowhere near finished but we could move in and save the rent I was paying here. After Viv and the new baby had been home for a couple of weeks and I had started work on the ruin for Judy, the lady who was leaving for the Alps, I began looking for an opportunity to speak to Viv about moving.

This was it! She was sitting on the terrace, breast feeding whilst drinking a cup of tea and reading a book. I took a cup and saucer outside, sat opposite her, poured myself out some tea and started to strike up a gentle conversation hoping to catch her unaware. No chance!

"Lovely day, Viv!" I said and leant back nonchalantly

"What do you want?" she said and put her cup down

"Nothing! Just having a chat," I said and looked puzzled

"You never chat, you're always plotting, so what do you want?"

"I was just going to say, when would you like to move into the house? It's almost finished and we wouldn't have to pay rent once there" I said and looked pathetic

"It's not almost finished! There's a lot to do before I would move in. You have work for at least six months, we will talk then."

"But the rent! It's hard to find it every month," I said and looked even more pathetic

"That's your problem, mine's bringing up three girls. You can swap if you want!" she said nodding at the bundle in her arms

"That's OK!" I said, poured myself another cup of tea and changed the subject.

I knew the real reason we were stalling, we didn't wont to leave the farm with Marcel and Evette, the life we had made, the happiness and little security we had came from this place, we didn't wont to leave the two people who made us feel we belonged. The children loved it here, I didn't wont to move them again, we didn't wont to move.

When I had first gone to see Judy's house it was a shock.

The house, as she called it, was in a very deserted position,

placed on top of a hill at the end of a long and exposed muddy track. The views looking out across the Pyrenees were wonderful. In the distance, small villages perched on top of soft hills, their church spires silhouetted against the sunny, blue sky.

But this place was even more isolated than mine. After getting out of her car and being led over to a pile of stones, I said:

"Where's the house?"

"There!" she said and pointed at the pile of rocks.

I tried to look over the stones to see the house.

"I can't see a house!" I said and turned back to look at her

"Well, it's not *exactly* a house," she said and looked down

"No, it's four walls that look like a pile of rocks! There's no roof or floors, no doors or windows," I said and gaped at the thing she called a house

"Well, if you got a roof on, then perhaps it would look a bit more like a house!" she said with determination.

f

She smiled and said:

"I knew you would accept this as a challenge,!"

I knew that meant she hadn't much money, but it was work anyway.

"Can you come over and look at my chickens?"

It was furry boot's husband, Steve.

"Chickens! Look at chickens! Why?"

"Two reasons: one, they can sing 'Three blind mice'; and the second is they have to go into the pot. I've never done that part of it. You've had lots of times on the farm, so I thought you could show me!"

"Sure! When?" I said, proud someone appreciated my new, agricultural knowledge

"Tomorrow night. The boys are away, and the wife's in bed with the 'flu," he said sounding conspiratorial, as if we were planning to decapitate little children

Furry boot's had lived alone the first year we had known her, we knew there was a husband in England and she kept saying he was on his way, but no one had materialised. Then one night she phoned and asked me over to meet him. The invitation was a surprise as I hadn't been told he was coming. And as the invitation was for me alone I realised I was supposed to become a mate of his, no doubt to encourage this reluctant emigrant to settle in a foreign land, I expected a bullish, hard, heavy, person, but instead was introduced to a thin, softly spoken, bearded young man, who was obviously drunk. Over the next few months I saw how painfully shy he was, I also thought him far to intelligent to live a life playing second fiddle to his wife, I hoped he had another plan, but feared the timid side of his personality would anchor him to the spot his wife had chosen for him, he buried his clever mind in alcohol, drinking twenty or more of the little bottles the super market sold very cheaply every day, I found him very likeable, and funny, if I could get him away from his wife, and before he got pissed.

"Write this down," I said, "get a big table and scrub it clean, a big pot with a gas ring underneath so we can keep the water hot, I will bring the magic powder. We will need loads of rags, string, hooks, bags for the feathers, bread crumbs and bits of bacon, a couple of very sharp knifes, and a long, thin, strong stick."

"What's the long, thin, strong, stick for?" he said nosily

"To conduct your singing chickens with. Oh yeah, one last thing, paint a red line around the top where the handle would be."

Then I put the phone down.

The next afternoon, I went over to his place and organised the layout of the Slaughter House, as his wife called it. The ritual was going to take place in his garage. We had got everything in place; the pot with the boiling water, the long flat table, the string strung out with hooks, the knives in place. I put the magic powder I had got from Marcel in a tub by the table. Then said to Steve:

"We can put the chickens in the pen over there, where the last owner kept his dogs," and pointed to the wired enclosure by his back door, " but first I want to see them sing!"

Steve went over to a dusty cupboard next to the boiling pot, opened it, took out a long, straight stick and held it up. Around the top he had painted a red line.

"What *do* you want this for?" he said, then handed it to me

"I'm legs and wings! This is for you,'" I said and handed it back

"Come on, I wont a cup of tea, then it's the birds' last performance!"

I went out to sit on his terrace; he went inside to make the tea.

The chickens were all perched in a tree growing up the side of his house. It was getting dark, and as the tree had no leaves on it yet, the birds were silhouetted against the sky. They were all squatting on their own branch, a black round ball of feathers with a beak.

'This lot are all fast asleep, how's he going to make them sing?' I thought.

Just then Steve appeared with a huge tray of tea and biscuits, for me and several bottles of beer for him. He put the tray on the table I was sitting at, then said:

"Pour your tea out and watch this!"

He went over to the garage then came back with a chair. He put the chair at the bottom of the tree holding the birds, climbed onto the chair, reached up to one of the chickens and squeezed it. It let out a small squawk. He then squeezed a few more, then moved his chair a foot to one side and squeezed the others. They all made a different squawking sound. He then turned round and faced me, rolled his sleeves up, bowed theatrically, turned back towards the chickens and started to squeeze them again; I soon realised the reason for the first squeezing session: he wanted to know which ones were making what noise, and what key it was in. Now his hands were flying around the tree squeezing different birds, in no particular order, except that the order he squeezed them in enabled him to make the squawks sound just like 'Three blind mice'! He was working franticly now, the bird orchestra singing quicker and quicker. It built up to a crescendo then the end came abruptly. The maestro's hands slumped to his sides, he turned slowly around, and bowed theatrically and deeply, I burst into loud applause. Steve jumped down from his chair, picked up a bottle of beer then downed it in one, I continued to clap, wonting more. He downed another bottle of beer, got back onto the chair, bowed towards me again, turned around and played Ten Green Bottles. After his and the chickens performance we sat around waiting for night time and darkness, Steve explained that once the chickens were roosted for the night they wouldn't move, that's how he could play them.

"I hope the next lot are as tuneful, because this lots in the pot tonight," I said and rolled my sleeves up.

We managed to get the chickens off the tree and into a box, six at a time. Eventually we had them all cooped up in the old dogs pen. It had become very dark outside; inside the garage had filled with steam and had become uncomfortably hot.

"Steve, open the garage doors, it's boiling in here!" I pleaded

"People will see what were doing," he said and looked guilty

"Steve, this is rural country. Everybody does this with chickens here; *open the doors*!"

He opened them and then glanced around outside.

"What you looking for? The French 'Save the Chicken Society?"

He came back inside, I told him to stand by the pot. 'All learners start there!' I thought.

I was going to duplicate everything Marcel had done with his geese. Went to the pen, took out a chicken and held it by its legs and wings, and walked over to Steve who had started to look sheepish.

"Don't let me down now, Stevey boy!" I said in my best American accent.

I held the bird out in front of me; its neck and head stuck out towards Steve.

"Take the stick, hold it at the end with the red ring, then hit it on the head, not too hard or its head will come off!"

Steve lifted the stick above his head.

"Not that hard! Just a decent tap, really," I commanded.

The stick was lowered to a sensible height, then a quick whack. The chicken's head swung down; in with the skewer behind the ear, then up onto the hook attached to the line. The plates were prepared with the bacon and breadcrumbs; I put this under the unconscious, bleeding bird.

"What's that for?" Steve said, gawping at the plate

"Your Misses, it's good for the flu," I lied

"You can give it to her!" Steve said and went and got another bird.

We worked away for the next hour. I had shown Steve how to put the powder on and wipe the feathers off, how to wash and clean the birds, tie them up, then put the carcasses in a line on the bench. We had about fifteen birds finished. The air was thick with the steam, and the smell of blood and drenched feathers. We had about five birds still hanging, one in particular had been awkward and although he was hanging like the others on the line he refused to give up and kept coming back to life. He would squawk and shake about hanging from his legs. I had given him several whacks on the head, but he still kept reviving himself.

We had just had a fag break and were about to start work again. Steve was reaching into the pen for the last of the chickens, I was standing in front of the hanging birds, scraping the blood off the table.

Steve jerked upright with no bird in his hand, turned towards me and started waving. I just stared at him, so he galloped over to me.

"There's someone coming along the path," he said panicking

"So what?" I said confused

"They're English! I can hear them talking," he said and started to move in front of the hanging chickens

"So what?" I said stupidly

"Imagine what they will see from their side of the door; it will look like a scene from the Texas chain Saw Massacre!" he said impatient at my short-sightedness

"Fuck! You're right!" I said and stood next to him to hide the sight of all the hanging chickens dripping blood onto plates of bread and bacon, "Not the thing for passing tourist to see, you're right mate!"

I squeezed closer to him.

"Wonderful night, darling! The stars are so bright," a well-spoken English gent was saying

"Beautiful! So glad we came. So quiet and serine," said a soft pretty voice.

I squeezed even closer to Steve as the voices became louder.

"There's smoke coming out of that garage door," the male voice said

"I think it's steam, dear. Let's look!"

'That's a woman!' I thought.

Two heads peered through the garage door and into the gloom, looking directly at us. A female voice said, in French:

"Are you making jam? Can we come in?"

Steve and I just stood very still.

The two heads didn't move in towards us, they were waiting for an answer. That chicken who refused to die was banging its head against my back. I had the stick in my hand behind me and was trying to whack it. The two heads were still smiling at us. Steve weakened.

"We're English," he stammered and waved his hand daftly.

The two heads came in carried by two smartly dressed gentle folk. I kicked Steve in the shin whilst trying to hit the bird on the head who had started to flapped its wings as well as jiggle its head.

At the sight of freshly killed naked chickens, lined up in a neat row along our bloody table, with a bucket full of bloody guts at the side of it, they both stopped in there tracks. The water pot started to boil ferociously, bubbling like an evil cauldron, Steve had forgotten to turn it down. Then unfortunately at that precise moment, the young lady put her delicate shoe onto one of the plates of semi-congealed blood; her little shoe sunk under the surface and covered her stockinged foot in sticky half congeled blood. She screamed and jumped backwards. The handsome, young man nodded apologies and bent down to look at her foot. The chicken behind my back had decided to give life one last go, let out a massive squawk and started to flap around over the top of my shoulder. At the sound of this the young man stood upright, the hook holding the chicken to the string slipped off as he straightened up. The chicken went sailing across the garage with its head flapping, blood squirting about all over the place, its flapping wings ran out of blood, then it flopped to the ground, landing with a thud on top of the young girls feet, it's blood squirting all over her stockings, she squawked louder then the chicken had, her young man grabbed her hand and bolted for the door, they disappeared out into the dark night, leaving one of her small shoes stuck in the blood pudding. Steve went over, picked up her shoe and wiped it clean, then said

"not exactly Cinderella,"

he then hung the guilty chicken back on the line, turned to me grinning,

"Wont a fag?" he said then started to laugh

"Did you see their faces?" I said clutching my sides, and fell on the floor.

Eventually, the work was completed and the garage spick and span. We decided to go to La Potou for an hour before bed; Steve's wife didn't like the idea, so I told her I had something to cure her 'flu. She was to put two spoonfuls in her tea in the morning. She thought it was something sweet.

Arrived at the bar expecting to see the usual assortment of farmers and drunks. On our entrance we were extremely surprised to find our young couple sat at the bar, they were startled to see us, we quickly explained to them what we were doing in the garage and why, then asked the jockey to go to the celler for a bottle of his vintage wine,

"You must think us both wimps," said the young lady taking a sip from her glass,

"You must think us both mad," answered Steve,

"Good job they didn't see the Singing Chickens, then," I said

and raised my glass,

"To Cinderella and the Singing Chickens," Steve called

"To two mad Cockneys from the Corbiéres," toasted the handsome young man

"To Coitus Couples and Countless Kids," I said joining in

"To Chickens, and Wimps, and Cockneys," said the pretty girl, then raised her glass, then emptied it .

"I've got your shoe in the car," Steve told our young lady, no doubt hoping he could put it on for her, she scrawled up her nose and said,

"it's o.k. thanks I have several pairs with me,"

It was there honey moon so they didn't stay to long, they enjoyed the wine and laughed at the night's events, looking at them I realised how rustic I was becoming, my cloths were old and dusty and the same colour as the countryside. My hands were bigger know, calloused and cut, I had become physicaly larger, through all the hard work. I had started to distrust men who didn't work with there hands or keep animals or grow some food, most of the time some part of me hurt, I was proud to be able to handle hard physical work, and since giving up drink my head worked quicker and my body worked slower. The wine drunk our young couple left, we walked them to there car, watched them drive off into the night and away to the big town

"I'm home sick," I told Steve

"I need a beer," he said walking towards the jockey.

## CHAPTER EIGHT

Our lives took on a gentle routine. The new baby, Georgina, brought nappies and breast feeding back. Viv slept with the baby and me in the spare bed. Victoria and Keira were maternal, but we had to be careful to give them both individual attention which was always a pleasure now. Walks up to perfume park became more frequent. Me and my two girls sat for hours amongst the herbs and spices in our little patch of perfumed wonder, talking about the things we could see around us and how the colours of the countryside altered during the four seasons. On some of our trips up there, we began attempting to reproduce the sights we loved by covering canvases with various coloured paints, using our hands and brushes. Then we returned to Viv with the canvases covered with delicious, oily landscapes smelling of linseed. We all agreeing they were 'really good' and Viv immediately hung them on the walls in our small house.

Victoria was riding with me more often, and Keira had started the piano, even though she couldn't reach the pedals. I went to work on Judy's house everyday, rode my horse, tended the vegetable patch and joined a cricket team in Toulouse. We had made French, British, Swedish, and Dutch friends and had more of a social life here than we'd had in England. Although we couldn't get out, people were always over for dinner or drinks.

The days passed in a happy, blissful haze of domesticity.

I had also bought another car, a Fiat that was at least a million years old. It was a white estate car that furry boots had been driving around for years. We had to get another car as Viv couldn't be left on the farm all day on her own. That bashed up old car would take me to work every day, as long as I took it nice and steady. I managed to get insurance for it and an MOT, but I knew if the police saw it on the road they'd pull it over and as I had no driving licence I didn't want that. The old thing would even take me into town to load up with building materials it wasn't worth the yard delivering. It staggered back, coughing smoke and belching oil, protesting at the extra weight it had to carry. I even started to attach that trailer to the back of it, making it tow loads as well. Every day I expected the old thing to sink into the tarmac never to rise again, yet every day when I turned the key it shook itself violently into life, spitting balls of black smoke out of its exhaust pipe. Then it juddered along the first few miles until its nuts and bolts had fallen into place, and off we sped on one more days work.

On one of these frosty mornings, the Fiat had been very difficult to start. I had pushed her to the brow of the village hill then pushed her over, jumped in the driver's door, we began to roll down the step hill, picking up a good speed. I pushed the gear lever into third, then released the clutch. The Fiat leapt forward and I felt the engine come into life, so I pushed my foot hard down onto the accelerator. A great cloud of thick, inky coloured smoke poured out of the back. The engine started to die, so I rammed my foot down harder on the accelerator then looked up, and saw the bend at the end of the lane looming towards me. The road started to go up, I swung the steering wheel around hoping to navigate the curve. Then, just as I was making the turn, the engine started to die again so I pushed my foot on the accelerator once more. Sooty smoke billowed from the exhaust pipe, but at least I had power! Through the dark smoke surrounding the car I saw three Gendarmes waving at me to stop.

"What the fuck are they doing there?" I said out loud.

The Fiat was slowing down towards them. The smoke cleared a little as one of the Gendarmes bent slightly at the hips, peering into the front window screen. A look of recognition passed over his face. He straightened up, then started to wave me on. I pushed the accelerator down carefully not wanting to cover them all in soot. I recognised the one who waved me on; sometimes when I picked Keira up from her nursery, he was there to pick his little girl up too. Once or twice he had been late, so I had stayed around to keep a quiet eye on her. He knew what I was doing, and there became a unspoken agreement between us that if one was late the other would hang around for a bit. He obviously saw at once the car was a mess and would get me into trouble, so waved me on. I felt like a local, and to my surprise it felt good.

Whenever I was out in the vegetable patch at night, Marcel came out for a chat. This particular night he seemed on edge and a little bit uneasy. He wanted to know if our house in the village was finished and if so when were we going to move in. I explained that Viv still wanted lots more work completed before she would leave here. To my surprise Marcel didn't readily accept this. He became slightly aggetated, sctatched his head then asked me what more work was there to do; I told him about the list Viv had given me, he looked confused. I had thought they would have been happy to have us stay here for as long as possible. Listning to Marcel I realised something was wrong. I started to wonder if they had other people they wonted to let the house to, Marcels manner made me wonder, he left as abrubtly as he arrived.

I knew nothing had changed between us, what ever Marcel was thinking, it would be for the better for us. I couldn't understand why he was so mystified about Viv wonting more work completed on the house before she would move, what difference to him? I had to think like him to understand, I started to put myself in his position, what would Marcel do in my place, then it was obvious.

He would never waste money on rent when he had a house to live in. As I was doing something nonsenseical he would think I had a reason, ether to sell the house and leave, or there was something going on that was wrong, I had to have a reason to pay rent and own a empty house. to Marcel, me paying rent to his son and owning a house was either stupid or suspicious.

I couldn't tell him we didn't really want to leave him or his beautiful farm, and that I suspected Viv's refusal to move was for the same reason. He would think that silly and expensive, a waste of money. I wondered if the other people in the village thought the same. 'yes they properly did' I reckoned

I realised it was time to leave.

'This old man was right, as usual.'

That night ,I didn't ask Viv about leaving and moving into the village, I told her. Because of money and common sense. There was no choice.

We agreed to make the move slowly, all of us visiting and staying in the house more often, and even starting to spend some nights there. I decided to have a week off work, to make the beds we would need and get the kitchen ready as far as possible. Then, with beds, a table to eat on, the kids acclimatised to the place, we could move in.

I worked furiously for three weeks, and still the house felt cold and empty.

At the end of the second week, I took Viv down to the house for an inspection. She looked around quickly, as if she had already made her mind up.

"Its fine darling, don't look so worried! Summer's here and the kids will be outside most of the time. Marcel's only five minutes away. Think of the rent we will save!"

"I know but I'll miss so many things from the farm. I'm terrified to lose this life we have found. I'm afraid we will leave the happiness on the farm with Marcel."

"Robert, *we* have our feelings, not Marcel! He only helped bring them out in us. We love them both, but will leaving stop that? *No*, just as it won't stop how you feel now, we have this beautiful house now, and dreams to look forward to",

Viv said and looked happy.

I knew she was right but I couldn't feel happy. Just nervous.

The work on Judy's house had gone well but had been a real challenge, I had enjoyed this one, there was nobody following me around, no begging for wages, I was left to design the place and build it as I liked, there had been days when the only way to keep warm was by putting my hands on the electric kettle, this was more than compensated by the hours I spent on my own, working out every new challenge, then watching the house take shape.

One late spring evening arriving home from work I saw bundles outside the front door. I had seen these bundles before, I knew what they meant: we were leaving.

I walked past the tied-up cartons and tucked up bales, and went into the vegetable patch. I went over to the seat I had made to rest on, looked at the new shoots appearing through the ground and rested my head in my hands. I started to think about the time we had spent here, all the adventures and laughter, the work, the fury, pain, love, birth, blood, soil and beauty, I sat listening, to the sounds of the farm.

Daydreaming happily and feeling contentedly sad.

There was a rustling behind me, I jumped up.

Marcel appeared from the side of our house and walked through the chicken wire gate into the vegetable patch.

"I see you're off soon," he said and sat down.

"Yes," I said and sat next to him.

He was looking down at my row of bright green seedlings, I sat waiting for him to talk.

"Robert I want to tell you something about living in the village, it's something I learnt a long time ago.

After the war I left Villautou and moved to Plavilla, I went to live with my twin brother, I was very sick and he would help me recover, I stayed there several years. Now as you know I was born in this village yet when I returned I was treated as a stranger, and I have never really forgiven them for doing that, you have lived up here on the farm for several years, you are one of *us*, the thing is, only make friends from three villages away, then if you fall out you don't have to see them. Wait two years before you let any strangers into your house. Nobody will help you down there, so don't help them. I am always here to talk to and Yvette is always here for Viveka, the children are welcome here at any time, I will miss them badly," he said all this quickly, as if he had rehearsed it several times, he stood up stretched, walked over the my newly sprouting potatoes and said

"all this lot's yours, come up and collect whrn you won't, get your new vegetable patch going straight away you're a bit late already, I will be up with the tractor in the morning and help with the move, come down for coffee as soon as Viv's ready."

Although this speech was made to help me better, instead it made me feel nervous, and realise how much he had protected us from.

The next day his tractor and trailer were throbbing outside our front door. The kids were throwing packages up to Marcel, I loaded our cars up, Yvette and Viv were buzzing around everywhere. Woolfy was running around with his tail high in the air grinning his big head off, this was excitement and action to him and he was not going to miss a second of it. Viv had of course cleaned every thing, washed the clothes, scrubbed all the pots and pans until they gleamed, crockery and her new bit's and pieces as she called them were all tidily padded and packed, everything in order and made to look neat and tidy. Marcel organised the packing of everything, Yvette organised the children and cleaned the cars out so I could get more in. The sun shone, the air smelt of spring flowers and was thick with pollen and blossom, a perfect day to leave. Then all loaded up, of course Marcel lead the way, sat up on his tractor, with the trailor hooked on to the back, the kids perched onto the top of the bags and bundles loaded onto the trailor, Evevette sat down clutching the two of them, the baby in thePeugeot with Viv, she never let any new born further then six inches away from her arms, the black bags packed so tightly in the back compartment they pressed against the windows, then me in that bashed up Fiat, laden with my gardening equipment and building tools. Marcel stood up, looked back over his shoulder, waved us forward then sat down. Black smoke shot over his head then off we went! The small column of smoking bumbling vehicles twisted slowly down to the village, the girls and Evette, laughing and waving the whole time.

A small line of anciant vehicles all blowing out smoke and squawking adults and children, Marcel drove slowly and carefully down the steep twisting bends then as he started to climb the hill a ball of black and white smoke shot into the air above his tractor as his foot pressed down onto his accelator.

We arrived into the empty village, filling it with our cavalcade of bouncing belongings, the children jumped down off the tractor and started to unload, swinging parcels and packages into their new home, we unloaded the cars and put everything into the big kitchen, Viv and myself immediately realised what little furniture we had. Trio appeared grinned at Marcel and said welcome back to us, Marcel looked at him and scowled. We all danced into Viv's kitchen, sat at the new table I had made while Viv started to make the coffee. After Viv put all the coffee things on the table I went to our only kitchen cabinet and took out a bottle of yellow stuff (whiskey) poured three small drams for the boys, and glasses of wine for the girls, gave the children the chocolate I had bought for the occasion, then raised a toast to our new home.

"To your new life, to peace and happiness," Marcel said and looked at Trio.

"Here's to our new neighbours and friends," Trio said and squawked at Marcel.

The coffee and drinks drunk, Marcel, Yvette and Trio left.

The girls were so excited they ran from room to room inventing a different game for each, the baby slept through all this. Viv set about her new kitchen with a fury. I walked out of the kitchen and into the garden, I had marked out a position for my new vegetable patch, I knelt down and picked at the soil, it was good stuff better than the farm, I squeezed the earth between my fingers and felt better about leaving my old vegetable patch, this one would do much better, less wind, flatter, and easier to water. Then I made a seat of stones and moss sat down and listened to the sounds of the excited house that was coming alive again after years of lonelyness, I could almost see it shacking itself in disbelief, it had a family to look after at last, the tinkling sound of childrens laughter bounced around the walls inside our new house of dreams. As the house quietened down, the sound of the children was replaced by the songs of roosting birds, chroking frogs and rustling trees. Viv appeared from her new kitchen carrying a tray of tea and sandwiches. She made a temporary table from some discarded packing boxes, covered them with a flower patterned table cloth she had under her arm, put the tea things in the order she wanted them, then poured.

"It's lovely here! Look at the snow on the mountains, and the green hills in front of them; there's not a pylon in sight! There's less wind here then on the farm, and we have complete privacy, you're to get the vegetable patch going as soon as you can, the children hate supermarket veg, and then you are to sort this garden out, and we have to have a terrace in front of the kitchen, I want to be able to see the baby playing outside, we have to plan for the summer, I think my parents might come to see us, I hope the man who drives the school car remembers I told him to come *here* tomorrow

" This view hasn't changed for centuries, I said and leant back on my stones,

"We'll be happy here," nice and quiet for a while before we go back to England"

I mused.

"Yes but before then, I want the house painted terracotta. I hate Tompierre, there's chickens as well, Victoria wants a chicken coup, Keira wants....

I put my arm around the back of her chair and nustled up against her, closed my eyes and let the setting sun and Viv's words warm my face.

Fini

Lightning Source UK Ltd.
Milton Keynes UK
UKHW040953030719
345495UK00001B/27/P